No Box Can Hold

No Box Can Hold

A Modern Study of Identity and Self-Discovery

Unique Ink Publishing
Roosevelt High School
Portland, Oregon

No Box Can Hold
A Modern Study of Identity and Self-Discovery

Copyright © 2014 by Roosevelt High School. All rights reserved.

ISBN # 978-1-939957-02-3

www.rooseveltroughwriters.org/unique-ink-publishing

Unique Ink Publishing
Roosevelt High School
6941 N. Central St.
Portland, OR 97203
(503) 916-5260

Project Manager: Anthony Sylvester
Editors: Lara Carvin, Laura Foster, Melissa Gifford, Marcus Lopez, Amber May, Kate McPherson, Miranda Mendoza, Melva Perez, Shannon St. Hilaire, and Doua Vang
Research: Anthony Sylvester, Kate McPherson, Melva Perez, and Nathan Buckland
Graphics: Nathan Buckland, Jeri Lee, Michael Cuauhtemoc Martinez, Bovianna Somsanouk
Photography: Julie Keefe, Kate McPherson, Renee Mitchell, Alissa Ouanesisouk, Melva Perez, Bovianna Somsanouk
Illustrations: Emily Biggs, Esperanza Chacon, Christie Jackson, Jeri Lee, Megan Lorenz, Michael Cuauhtemoc Martinez, Amber T. May, Miranda Mendoza, Molly Mendoza, Abby Pasion, Silvia Salinas, Daniel Stauffer, Blake Stellye, and Brenda Tirado

Cover Design: Anthony Sylvester and Diana Goodrich
Interior Design: Margaret Schimming

Permissions:

"Being Brown" by Jen Wick, used with permission by Oregon Humanities.

"The Negro Mother" from THE COLLECTED POEMS OF LANGSTON HUGHES by Langston Hughes, edited by Arnold Rampersad with David Roessel, Associate Editor, copyright ©1994 by the Estate of Langston Hughes. Used by permission of Alfred A. Knopf, an imprint of the Knopf Doubleday Publishing Group, a division of Random House LLC. All rights reserved.

"Ego Tripping" by Nikki Giovanni used with permission, ©1968 Nikki Giovanni.

"Still I Rise," from AND STILL I RISE by Maya Angelou, copyright ©1978 by Maya Angelou. Used by permission of Random House, an imprint and division of Random House LLC. All rights reserved.

"Bill of Rights for People of Mixed Heritage" by Maria P.P. Root

For information regarding special purchases of *No Box Can Hold: A Modern Study of Identity and Self-Discovery*, contact Unique Ink at the address above.

All proceeds from the sale of this book support Roosevelt's Writing and Publishing Center.

Printed in the United States of America.

About this Book

No Box Can Hold is the second publication of Roosevelt High School's Unique Ink Publishing. Unique Ink is a student-led publishing center whose mission is to work with the community to publish regional pieces. Our diverse writers use the written word to express who they are. The publishing center will enable writers—young and old, novice and professional—to powerfully raise their voices.

Every year students will publish at least one book, providing the opportunity for Roosevelt students to:
- Share their writing with the larger community
- Work with professionals and college students to write, edit, design, and market the publication.
- Apply their writing skills to all elements of project communication and management
- Generate revenues to sustain the Writing and Publishing Center at Roosevelt High School

---

This summer's internship has been a really big and important step in my life as a high school teenager. I gained many new and helpful skills, and I was faced with challenges that I overcame thanks to the people around me. The fears I had at the beginning of the internship are slowly vanishing.
—Melva Perez, Unique Ink summer intern

The 2013 Unique Ink Summer Internship gave enterprising Roosevelt students a chance to be part of creating a real publication. In partnership with Ooligan Press of Portland State University, these interns began to formulate a purpose and direction for the book you are about to read. They gathered submissions from fellow students, professional authors and community members. They practiced and learned skills involving writing, editing, revising, marketing, and design. They were introduced to working in a professional atmosphere. They worked with computer programs such as InDesign and Photoshop to make visuals and marketing tools for the book. The lessons learned during the summer will stay with them through high school and into college, and their names are immortalized in the pages of this book.

Roosevelt's Writing and Publishing Center

Where Writing Transforms Our Selves and Our Futures

We believe developing strong, confident writers who proudly express their beliefs and knowledge and who value continuous improvement is central to effectively preparing students for college and life. We have designed the Roosevelt High School Writing and Publishing Center to:

- Enhance academic writing skills for graduation, college and career
- Raise attention to young voice and writing in the community
- Sustain our near-peer mentoring opportunities and the Roosevelt Writing and Publishing Center itself.

A diverse team of well-trained high school and college students provide one-on-one and small group writing consultation. We hope that our efforts in collaboration with teachers at RHS will enable students to meet the required writing proficiency and prepare them for articulating their thoughts as students, workers, and citizens.

Modeled on college writing centers, the RHS center familiarizes students with a resource that will also help them succeed in college.

Student writing is richer and more interesting when it has a real purpose. Roosevelt's Publishing Center helps student writing come alive as it is shared and influences the community in positive ways.
—Charlene Williams, Senior Director of School Performance, Roosevelt Cluster|Benson High School

Roosevelt's Writing and Publishing Center creates an important space for students to discover, refine, and share their voices. Our students learn about themselves and their communities through writing and share their stories with the world at large.
—Filip Hristić, Principal, Roosevelt High School

The Writing Center helped me refine my scholarship essays so they were more focused and powerful.
—Warren Vang, Gates Millennium Scholarship Winner

The Writing and Publishing Center is a program of Roosevelt's College and Career Transition Center. Learn more about the Center and its programs at www.rooseveltroughwriters.org.

It is my honor to present to you the essence of our community through this collection of poems and prose pieces that reflect the process of finding identity. This is a perilous and exhausting journey, but it is also wonderful and gratifying. People identify with different morals, beliefs and ideas, and it is because of this we live in a world so beautiful, with variety and freshness. This book just scratches the surface of this deep concept, but its representation of the Roosevelt and Portland community is what makes it special.

I hope you will take time to read through this publication, and see the world through eyes other than your own. Maybe you will find something that speaks to you and changes you forever, for the better.

Congratulations to the Roosevelt students for putting this publication together and good luck to you on your own personal journeys.

Charlene Williams
Senior Director of School Performance
Roosevelt Cluster|Benson High School

Keep in mind that though searching for our identities is an internal process, many external factors come into play. Parents teach us about our cultures and help us to embrace our heritage. The journey to find our own sense of self is difficult and painful, but the blow can be softened by feeling that we belong somewhere. Also, understand that we need to push back against you in order to become more independent. Our rebellion is not an act of spite or hate but rather a side effect of the struggle we endure everyday of growing into young adults, and it is necessary for us to progress as individuals. Embrace us when we need help and respect us when we need space. Think back to when you were our age and remember your own struggle. It isn't easy, but hopefully this publication will spread some light on a subject shrouded in mystery and misunderstanding. Join us on our journey.

Anthony Sylvester
Project Manager

Contents

About this Book		v
Roosevelt's Writing and Publishing Center		vi
Introduction		1

Age and Development
Easy Math	Amber T. May	4
Tit for Tat	Christi Krug	7
It's All in My Head	Mary Jane Haake	11
She Never Forgets	Francis McCollister	13

Culture and Ethnicity
Detribalized Aztec	Michael Martinez	16
Gadugi	Duane Poncy	18
South Dakota	Leah Gibson	19
Longing to Belong	Leah Stenson	21
Islander	Melva Perez	23
The Culture Jar	Brenda Tirado	25
Asta la Victoria	Jaime Guzman	28
Forgotten History	Roman Rocha	29
Fly	Lucía Gaspar	32
Volar (translation of Fly)	Lucía Gaspar	34
A Home in Two Countries	Espoir Mbirize	37
Conversation	Doua Vang	42
Masterpiece	Walidah Imarisha	45
Blended Culture	Nathan Buckland	49

Mindset
Torn	Shandi Borchin	52
Who am I?	Debra Mendoza	54
Still I Rise	Maya Angelou	56
Born Again	Isaac Kelly	58
Don't You Know Your Worth?	Ania Warren	61
I Look in the Mirror	Faith K. Lao	63
Let Me Introduce You	Silvia Salinas	64

Disability
Narrative	Travis Koski	68

And Proud	Josh Howe	70
To Be a Roughrider	Jonathan Alex Rogers	71
The Strong One: A Conversation with Brenda L. Dailey	Amber T. May	72

Gender and Sexuality

What is Tattooed on Me with Invisible Ink	Zoe Senner	76
The Box	Wesley Cady	78
Heels	Loretta Stinson	80
My First Manifesto	Victoria Braun	83
Mating Call of the Great Northern American Bisexual Homo Sapiens	Jocelyn Loyd	84
To Inhabit the Body	Willa Schneberg	87
About Me and You and Us	Amanda Saenz	88

Relationships

If You Leave	Emily Nowlin	92
Snowball	Troy May	93
Unwanted Born Life	Madison Parks	95
Poisonous Fantasies	Lara M. Carvin	96
Family or Mami?	Diana Villalobos	98
Sisters' Sonnet	Rachel Pass	100
A Letter to My Adoptive Mother	Ellen Brahe	102
Seeing Things	Cindy Williams Gutiérrez	104

Race

Bill of Rights for People of Mixed Heritage	Maria P.P. Root	114
The Painted Victim of a Bleached Society	Jocelyn Loyd	115
Skin	Willa Schneberg	116
Define Me	Alex Gerald	117
The Accidental Racist	Ari Abramovitz	121
We're all the Same	Cesar Pineda	123
Just Because	Sean Miles	125
Give Me Some Skin: How I Became White	Patrick McDade	127
The Negro Mother	Langston Hughes	130
Coffee	Justin McDaniels	133
Remembering Race	Cindy Williams Gutiérrez	134
Ego Tripping (there may be a reason why)	Nikki Giovanni	136

Lost	Miranda Mendoza	139
White Guilt	S. Renee Mitchell	142

Religion

The Red Road to Home	Brenda Reyes	148
I Didn't Ask for This.	Brooke Perry	150
Third Chance	Jake Peru-Bass	154
The Hijab	Qanani Kalil	156
Identify Our Oneness	Arun Toke	158

Spark

O Identity, What Art Thou?	Doc Macomber	162
The Pen is as Mighty as the Paintbrush	Abby Pasion	164
Football Life	Mendel Miller	165
The Curtain	Devin St. John	167
My Basketball Life	DaLony Armstrong	169
Passion for the Action	Melissa Vang	170
The Choir	Vikram Srinivasan	171
A Thousand Words	Julio Lopez	173
On Stage	Allissa Purkapile	174
The Trinity Seesaw	C.J. Rue	175
My First Love	Alissa Ouanesisouk	177

Thoughts and Reflections   179

What Our Peers Need to Know	180
What Our Parents Need to Know	181
What Our Teachers Need to Know	182

Acknowledgements   184

Introduction

Melva Perez

Every day, we try to be ourselves. In the modern world, we are exposed to many things. We go through different experiences, meet different people and find different passions all while discovering ourselves. From our skin color, religion, sexuality, culture, and "spark" we can find the things that make us "us." We lose who we truly are when we let people influence us or put us down, physically or verbally.

Lots of new ideas that used to be looked down upon have become everyday situations today. Same-sex marriage is slowly becoming more accepted, women are playing big roles just as men are, and interracial couples are very common. We are very open to things that our culture would've never considered or allowed a few decades ago.

Technology has played a big role in our generation. It's so advanced now that we can see the world in a blink of an eye. We explore all over the world. We see what "perfect" looks like around the world. It's making youth want to change to meet society's expectations. We are attached to our smart phones and social media. Using them on a daily basis has sucked us into almost losing connection from reality because we depend on them too much. Cyberspace is a whole different place and it will no doubt be a platform for identity.

Through this book, we encourage young people to develop a solid sense of their own identity so they can thrive in the world. We as young people are learning every day about who we want to be. The book helps show how identity shapes us. Living in the U.S., we are exposed to many things. The book shows people who have overcome obstacles of judgment or never fitting in. It seems sometimes there is never a correct place for a person, but knowing other perspectives helps us thrive.

Age and Development

Maturity is when your world opens up and you realize that you are not the center of it.

M.J. Croan

Adolescence is like having only enough light to see the step directly in front of you.

Sarah Addison Allen
The Girl Who Chased the Moon

Easy Math

Amber T. May

I have come to think of my youth as a kind of mythology.

The thick love of the heroines
    was their weapon their Zen,
the sadness of the villains
    was more terrifying
than their rage.
What happened to the little girl
    I was?
If I subtract 1981 from
whatever year it is...I see how
she became
me. So why do I mourn her?
If I try I can remember how all those days got filled.
    They are not lost.
So why do I regret and ache
for them
like an addict?

There is so much death before dying.

I think my lungs must have taken
air differently then, and expulsed it
in a manner more pleasing
    to the trees.
    I trusted
the journey,
    knew it was everything,
    basked
in it at its word and its silence.

    Today I'm losing faith,
not in that which I cannot see,
    but in that which I see daily.

I guess the closest metaphor is the caterpillar cocoon butterfly...

But in my case, I was the butterfly first.

By Julie Keefe

Tit for Tat

Christi Krug

I know what's happening the moment my cheeks fill with hot blood. I'm sharpening my pencil as a shaving alights on my arm, and I look up to see Sam Settlemeier standing close. He shakes the black hair from his eyes. He is staring at my chest.

I straddle the pencil sharpener to hide the two bumps rising above my ribs, round and pooching, like cookies from an Easy Bake Oven. None of the other girls have them, except Lisa May Robinson, but she is round all over so you don't notice.

Sam Settlemeier sharpens his pencil, sits down at his desk, and whispers, "Penny's got tits."

It wouldn't be so bad having my body be different if I wasn't already different in other ways. Other kids without dads are Ruby Nickels, with a divorced dad in Oregon, and Cara Rosenbaum, who gets taken out for ice cream by her divorced dad, and Tanya Parkin, whose mom has a boyfriend who is dad-like. I'm the only kid in fourth grade with a dad who's dead.

I start wearing baggy shirts. I pull my hair forward, over my shoulders, trying to cover my chest. I can't get a comb through it. Neither can Mother.

That's the other thing that makes me different. Mother isn't like other mothers. She gets sick a lot, at least that's what they call it, but it's not the regular kind of sick where you stay in bed. It's the kind of sick when you talk to people who aren't there, and get tired, and can't do normal things like drive a car or make dinner.

Anyway, I tell Mother to leave my hair alone. I wash it myself in the kitchen sink, with Breck shampoo, on Monday.

The luckiest girls in my class are Kathy, Mary, and Lisa May Robinson. They get Hostess fruit pies in their lunchboxes. They wear different shoes different days. They jingle rainbow bracelets. At recess, they play this game under the giant pine tree called Horses, which sounds like a little kid game, but really, it isn't. They have technique. They curl their knuckles underneath their hands, stretching wrists tall as hooves as they prance on all fours. They only invite you to play if they like you.

The swings are a better choice, anyway. Your knuckles don't get sore.

On Tuesday, Sam Settlemeier turns around in recess line like he's going to say something, but Lisa May Robinson gets in front of him. She reaches out and fingers a swatch of my hair. "It's so long and pretty," she says.

I wash it Wednesday and Thursday.

On Friday, I look in the dirty clothes pile. There's only one shirt, the tight blue one that stretches all the way down the waist and snaps at the crotch.

"Look at that," Sam Settlemeier whispers to Juan, at reading. "I see Penny's nips."

My pencil is getting shorter and shorter, but I stay at my desk.

Brad McFay says to Peter, "Have you noticed Penny's tits?"

If I press down hard I can make the pencil work.

"I can barely read your writing," Mr. Boggs writes in red pen on my spelling paper.

I need help, but there's nobody.

"Christy. Christy Penny!" calls Lisa May Robinson at recess. She scoops air with her arm, motioning me to the giant pine tree. Oh, this is good. The swings are getting boring.

I walk up and Lisa May Robinson says, "What you need is a bra."

It's not a word Mother uses.

"You have to *tell your mom* to take you shopping," she says, like she's spelling out a word for someone who doesn't know anything, even though I'm a better speller than she is.

Kathy and Mary are neighing and cantering with technique. I don't get down on all fours and prance upon the soft needled earth. I'm the one with tits, even though I'm not as round as Lisa May Robinson.

When I come in from recess my face is red, I know. Maybe people will think it's the rush of air, from all my time on the swings.

"Mother," I tell her after school, in one big breath so I can get it out, "I need a bra."

"You do?" She looks up from her magazines and pillboxes. Her bare feet rest on the ripped vinyl chair. She bites her lip. "Oh."

She blinks like a person waking up. "Well, then, you do."

She'll take days to make it happen, and there will be awful waiting and fussing, out in public, where other people will know that I'm different because I have a different mother, and there's nothing I can do about it. "You have to take me shopping right away," I say.

"Yes," she says. "Of course."

We catch one bus, then another, getting off at Fifth and Pine, Frederick & Nelson.

"Excuse me," Mother says to the man at the counter. There are tables with shoes and potted ferns. "I'm looking for young women's undergarments."

I want to die already. "We're in Fine Footwear," I whisper to Mother, yanking her away.

"Up the escalator, and then turn right, past Better Sportswear," the man says.

"Christy!" calls Mother. "Christy!" Her voice shakes with panic, like I really did die.

I'm huddled by some buckled boots and plastic daisies. "Shhhh! I'm right here!"

At the top of the escalator she looks around. "Well, there's Better Sportswear. I don't see any undergarm—"

I grab her hand. "This way!"

There are racks and racks of underwear and bras. The bras are lacy and long, enormous. What are you supposed to do with the straps?

A lady is sliding bras along a silver rack. "Excuse me," Mother says. "We're looking for a Beginner Brassiere."

Even my toenails are sweating.

"Sorry, I don't work here," says the lady.

Mother plods toward chunky silver letters on the wall: *Lingerie*. Here by the fake fern, perfume is lingering, taking all the oxygen out of the air. A sales lady swishes up to us. "May I help you?"

"My daughter needs a brassiere," says Mother.

"A training bra?" The lady looks at me. And looks.

What I could do is turn around. Go down the escalator and catch a bus and get on another bus and go home and wear my coat indoors all year, without any training at all.

And I'll tell Mr. Boggs, "My aunt bought me this coat the day she died and I can't bear to take it off." Or, "I was born in the Arizona desert and I've never gotten used to the cold." Or, "My skin is allergic to the spring air. It gives me hives."

Those stories would make me feel less different, but I know I won't really say anything. I'll just sit at my desk and feel the burning in my face.

The lady takes three training bras off hangers and puts them in my hands. Mother follows me to the Lingerie Dressing Room. "I can do this myself! Please!" I shut the door.

I take off my shirt, green with stripes. Lisa May Robinson gave me this shirt as a hand-me-down. I hope it looks better on me than it did on her.

My tits are the whitest things, like they're surprised. I cover them up. This bra is too lacy. This one, too big. The next one, okay.

The bra looks like maybe it's supposed to be there, and maybe the tits are supposed to be there, too.

"I want the one with the white bow," I announce when I come out.

"Good," Mother says. "I'm trying on a brassiere. You can wait for me on this bench."

There's a display table with a tower of striped boxes of Frango mints. There is a small waterfall over by the escalator. Ballet violin music plays over the speakers, but the matching song in my head is:

> On top of spa-ghet-ti! All covered with cheese
> I lost my poor meatball, when somebody sneezed

Then all at once there's a pounding in the dressing room.

"Help me! Somebody!" comes the voice. It's her, spazzing out over something any other mother could handle. Freaking for the umpteen billionth time.

A doorknob rattles. "Get me out!" *Thump, thump, thump.*

The saleslady walks up to the dressing room door where Mother is. I sit with my face in my hands. The saleslady's perfume clogs my throat.

The lady turns a key in the silver doorknob. Mother stands there with her big boobs and white pointy bra and white stomach and panty hose, taking gulpy breaths. "Oh! I thought I was locked in!"

"You just needed to turn the knob," said the lady.

The next time I need to go shopping, I take the dollars from Mother's purse, and walk to the drugstore. Underneath my green shirt, I'm wearing my bra with the white bow. I can do this thing myself. I mean, I've got tits.

It's All in My Head

Mary Jane Haake, Age 61

Before Norman Sylvester, the blues musician known as the "Boogie Cat," asked me to participate in Anthony Sylvester's writing project, I had never really considered my unique personality and DNA. My examination exposed patterns I'd never before noticed. I was too busy living my life like a gerbil in a wheel. By stopping the dance and looking inward, I gained insights that changed the way I will live from here on out—and it may change your viewpoint as well.

My first memories involve the advent of kindergarten. At age five, I identified with my thumb. I was a thumb sucker, a clever one. I knew enough to keep it hidden from the nuns and my mother. This appendage was my solace, a friend that had a calming influence as I entered an entirely new social structure. I was poor, short, snaggle-toothed and freckle-faced. My thumb saved me.

Ten years later, I identified with Joan of Arc, burning with religious fervor. Being the shortest person in class meant I got to lead the May Procession every year, and I was convinced God had chosen me to be His one and only. I was beginning to learn that what is a deficit one day is an asset the next. The nuns groomed me to join the order of the Sisters of the Holy Cross. While my adult eyes would have seen them as poor Irish women with no options, at the time I viewed them as all-powerful. No wonder I identified with them so strongly.

By my late teens and early twenties, I identified with Della from Perry Mason, the old TV drama about an all-knowing lawyer. She was his secretary, but so much more. She hid guns in her purse for him, sat in on every client conference and attended every trial, taking notes and offering Perry sage advice. I was sure she and Perry were having an affair and he would eventually make an honest woman of her. She was worldly and knowing. I was neither. I went to paralegal school, worked in a law office and looked for a suitable "Perry" of my own. When I eventually found him and got married, I discovered that I'd related to Della's role as a strong single woman and not the Della that was a compliant traditional wife.

I spent the next ten years running from traditional married life. Now I identified with hippies and outsiders. I wove my own wool, made my own clothes, grew my own food, made my own art. Living in Florence, Italy, in a tiny third floor room with no heat or bathroom, I flaunted my poverty. When I actually became a successful artist, I hid it from the public. I chummed around with punk artists and subversive writers. I was off the books, off the beaten path, off the charts.

As I transitioned into adult life, I identified with the painter Frida Kahlo. I painted, wrote screenplays, and ran a small tattoo studio tucked away in the sunny corner of an aging downtown office building with no visible signage. I was in the open but unseen. As my blood family distanced themselves in shame, I found a new family—my collectors and fellow artists. Together we built an ink and soul connection.

At the dawn of the 21st century, the Internet opened up the world to me. I identified with the entire planet, with Mother Earth. I now worked to facilitate funding my travel. A sense of urgency began to blink on the horizon. I felt a keen need to see environments before they were forever gone—and before I was.

Now, in my seventh decade, I identify with boundaries, real and imagined. I still open myself up to the world, but realize that evil exists. I lock my doors, but I also smile and nod a silent greeting to passersby. Time is precious and I desire to spend it with those who enhance my experience, and distance myself from any form of negativity. If that means not being polite or speaking up when I witness behavior unbefitting a polite society, I force myself to take that leap. I fear the lecture I would give myself later more than the aspect of reprisal. Once I can comfortably inhabit these new boundaries, I believe I will identify with the authentic me.

She Never Forgets

Francis McCollister

Remember me as the one who is shy but
constantly, (surprisingly) keeps going through every
struggle, every mean word, who stands up for what's right.

Who loves the world
but most times doesn't show it.
Who tries to show a smile but it keeps hiding
inside (who wants to let it out somehow).
Who admires her teachers, looks up to her friends

and loves her parents.
Never forgets that family is everything
and that life must go on—
so keep being strong
and unafraid to let out a tear
once in a while.

Culture and Ethnicity

A people without the knowledge of their past history, origin and culture is like a tree without roots.

Marcus Garvey

Culture is the process by which a person becomes all that they were created capable of being.

Thomas Carlyle

Detribalized Aztec

Michael Martinez (Aztec Name: Cuauhte'moc)

I miss home.
The desert air, warm and alive
with Tejano accordions and the sweet,
sweet smell of pan dulce.
Grandma's hugs—strong and
from the soul, as if all of my
ancestors embraced me:
From Olmeca to Méxicano-Tejano.
She's sleeping with Grandpa now.
A man whose bold voice, strong
back, and gentle manner harkened
back to the very first chiefs of Anáhuac:
The Basin of México.

¿Y yo?
Un Indio que quiere llorar.
Assimilation, anglicization, and the
loss of language, stifle me. I could
never understand the people that
I cared for most.
Mi familia—trampled by intolerance,
conquistadors, and all-American bigotry.

In the dingy missions, built by my hand
and my brother's hand
and our mother's land and
mortared with father's blood,
I was supposed to forget Tenochtitlán.
To accept a white god or to be impaled by a sword.
I was given nothing and treated
like dirt, and expected to splash around
on the beaches of Normandy. To be killed
in Korea and shot at in Vietnam.

They said, "Spanish is the language of
doormen, dishwashers, and fruit pickers."
And before that the friars hurled their
torches at our cities and pride,
and my Indian forebears cried,
"O weep my friends!
They are burning our library!"

Yes! I was supposed to forget my Tenochtitlán.
My Language.
My past.
But I long for that land,
and the sun.
The taste of breakfast tacos
and the aroma of soft, warm tortillas.
¡Ay mi linda familia!
I miss you.

Gadugi

Duane Poncy

In the old times, the Elders
in their ancient wisdom
knew that whoever belongs to Elohi
are fed by the blood of Selu. Our children sprout from her soil.

When grandmother became ill, the Healer brought herbs,
ceremonies and spells to ward away the Raven Mockers,
who hungered for the taste of her old, wise spirit.

The whole village came to harvest her sweet corn,
fat squash and pole beans. Came to store the bounty
in the old woman's cellar. This is Gadugi.

Now the people have forgotten the ceremonies and spells.
The Raven Mockers come, circling in their SUVs,
waving unpaid mortgages, to steal away life before its end.

South Dakota

Leah Gibson

I am learning to love and hate the smell of stale beer and
    sweetgrass
sage,
and hot tar pavement.

The smells of prairie and concrete,
like something was left out in the middle of nowhere
to rot and die, forgetting that
the something was us.

My people are here,
meaning those who have had my blood
running in their veins for centuries.

I search in their faces for traces of me.

I imagine my people strong and lean,
chasing buffalo across unending fields,

dark brown leathery skin,
hair jet black and long

nothing between here and there to stop us.

But these storefronts and buildings are cutting into my vision—
advertising beer and cigarettes and bingo,
stopping my people from running any further

to trap them
to make them fat and addicted.

Now the buffalo are long gone.

My people can see nothing outside square-house cell-windows,
fearing to venture outside the storefront walls alone.

I see my family in their faces
and pound fists against concrete,
wishing to smash their beer bottles
(that aren't really theirs or anyone else's here),
To raise the buffalo from the dead
and remind them of what it's like

to *run*.

Longing to Belong

Leah Stenson

I'll never forget the day that my six-year-old came home crying because a group of Japanese junior high school students in Tokyo had tauntingly called her *gaijin*. The kanji character for *gaijin* literally means "outside person," and for most foreigners living in Japan in the 1980s, the connotation of the word was far from positive. My daughter was distraught because she had always considered herself Japanese. She had been born and raised in Japan, spoke the language and attended Japanese nursery school.

After 16 years in Japan I returned to the United States. Instead of moving back to New York City, my former home, I moved to Portland, Oregon. Instead of feeling relieved to be "at home" in my own country at last, I was surprised to find that I felt out of place. Somehow I was different from the people around me. I had been told that I shouldn't expect people in the States to show an interest in or understanding of my experience of having lived abroad; however, I wasn't prepared to feel that, once again, I was an outsider. Sometimes people would say, "You're not from around here, are you?" At such times I had to make a conscious effort to not give in to feelings of negativity and alienation.

Hopefully, someday in the not too distant future, nationality will cease to be a human construction and the world's people will know in their hearts that they all belong to the same human race.

By Kate McPherson

Islander

Melva Perez

They say I look a certain race.
That I'm obviously different since my skin is darker.
What could she possibly be? Mexican?
Indian?
Black?
Mixed?
I say I'm neither.
Don't get confused with my last name.
Don't get confused with the bags under my eyes.
Don't get confused with my pigment.
I say I'm Islander. That's my ethnicity.
Oh, so you're from Hawaii?
You know how to play the ukulele?
You miss all those palm trees and beaches?
Can you speak your native language?
I really like eating pineapples and love hula dancing. It's so beautiful
    to me.
I say no.
No.
No.
No.
And negative.
I say I'm from an Island called Palau.
Hawaii is not the only island out on the Pacific.
I say I can play the ukulele but it's not the only instrument Islanders
    play.
I was never born and raised on sunny beaches with palm tree views.
I can't speak my language—only understand it.
They look confused now.
They ask with misinformed expressions how this can be.
Where is Palau?
Why call yourself an Islander when you're not born and raised?
You seriously haven't seen the surf and ocean waves?
Since you're from this island, you should be bigger physically.
We thought you qualified for free lunches.
Your parents make enough?

You're supposed to be fresh off the boat.
I say with a blunt face that I've heard it all.
You only think this because of television and other people's views.
Not all Islanders do these things. Mostly tourists do activities like
    that.
Not every Islander is big, especially not my people.
Micronesians are not close to what Hawaiians are.
And I'm an Islander because that's my ethnicity.
It's part of my character and personality.
Why do all this if you're not a true native?
I say that's the way I was raised.
Just because you're here
doesn't mean you have to act
exactly like you're from there.
I eat everything with rice.
I'm in love with all the little Asian markets in Portland.
I could wear sandals 24/7 if my parents didn't give a damn.
They taught me that my siblings and I are a legacy.
They came here for a better life but they stay true to Islander
    traditions.
We will be the last ones here, supporting and showing people
who we are and from where we originated
Then our children will keep it alive and their children and so forth.
The people can't say anything anymore.
They look pretty stunned. I probably went too far explaining myself,
but it's my voice. I mean I'm only human.
There's more than color and skin.
There's a brain. A speaking mind. Influenced
by its surroundings

There's more than what you know about it.

The Culture Jar

Brenda Tirado

As a sixteen-year-old, life is not always easy. I have not learned much, but I have learned enough to understand the two cultures I come from. I was born in the City of Roses, but I come from Mexico. I'm made of two cultures: Oregon and Aztec. In Oregon, a rose is the symbol and the rain visits very often. By contrast, Mexico is a totally different place where the sun burns through your skin, where you can have a drink with a straw from a plastic bag.

The last time I was in Mexico, I had to speak only Spanish, not English. Because I can't speak Spanish as well as they can, my friends tell me I'm a disgrace to my culture. This offends me a lot and makes me feel bad because they're right. Yet, when I am in Oregon, my friends toss around racist comments. They call me names like wetback and border hopper, and say that I do not belong here and should go back to Mexico. They say I have an accent when speaking English.

Some believe that being bicultural is silly or not possible. For me it is an honor to carry two different cultures in me. Why? Well, because I have the privilege of holding two cultures. I am a young, bilingual girl. It is a privilege to be surrounded by two communities that are very different but have something in common. And most importantly, I am the voice of both worlds. I am a sixteen-year-old who has two cultures in herself, growing and learning from them both. I'm like a jar where both cultures were mixed in, not split in half. I am filling the jar that keeps expanding, a mixture of my two cultures.

Para una adolecente de diesiséis años, la vida no siempre es fácil. Yo no hhabré aprendido mucho. pero he aprendido lo suficiente como para entender las dos culturas de las que vengo. Yo nací en la Ciudad de las Rosas, pero vengo de México. Estoy hecha de ambas culturas: la cultura de Oregon y la cultura Azteca. Oregon, un lugar en donde una rosa es un símbolo y en donde la lluvia visita muy amenudo. Por el contrario, México es un lugar totalmente diferente, donde el sol quema a través de la piel, donde se puede tomar un refresco con una pajita de una bolsa de plástico.

La última vez que estuve en México, tuve que hablar solamente en Español y no en Inglés. Porque no podía hablar en español tan bien como mis amigos, ellos me dijeron que era una a verguenza para mi cultura. Me ofendieron mucho, y eso me hizo sentir mal porque tenían razón, no podía hablar Español tan bien como ellos. Sinembargo, al estar en Oregon mis amigos hacen comentarios racistas y me ponen sobrenombres como espalda mojada, tolva de la frontera, dicen que no pertenezco aquí, que regrese a México y que tengo acento al hablar Inglés. Soy juzgada porque vengo de dos mundos diferentes.

Para aquellos que consideran que el ser bicultural es absurdo o que no es posible, yo les digo que para mi es un honor ser parte de dos culturas diferentes. ¿Por qué? Pues, porque tengo el privilegio de pertenecer a ambas. Soy una joven bilingue y es para mi un privilegio ser parte de dos comunidades que siendo tan distintas, tienen algo en común. Aún más importante, yo soy la voz de esos dos mundos. Soy una joven de diesiséis años que lleva ambas culturas en ella misma. Voy creciendo en ellas y enriqueciendome de ambas. Soy como el cántaro entero en donde dos culturas se han mezclado, no dividido en dos mitades y yo, voy llenándolo, expandiéndolo, transformándolo en laexperesión de esas, mis dos culturas.

By Kate McPherson

Asta la Victoria

Jaime Guzman

I am from undocumented dreams
I am from undocumented empowered dreams
I am from undocumented and unafraid dreams
I am from development, relief and education for alien minors
I am from DREAMers
I am from a movement of young leaders
I am from a group of youth and community that is not afraid
I am from building alliances to creating communities of trust and hope
I am from no more politics to activist
I am from negative energy turned into positive change
I am from where we don't criminalize our parents, rather, we admire and honor them
I am from not all undocumented youth are valedictorians and we are demanding to be heard
I am from where this is not a Latino's problem, it's our nation's problem
I am from where a nine-digit number doesn't exist
I am from where a paper doesn't make me human, I decide and own who I am
I am from sacrifices
I am from humor
I am from justice and equality
I am from asta la Victoria

Forgotten History

Roman Rocha

I was raised without a sense of cultural identity. My mother, aunts and uncles did not encourage cultural awareness, so early on I was not bombarded with many stereotypes: *You're Mexican; you should love beans. All Mexicans speak Spanish.* English was my first language and I looked at everyone as a person. It wasn't until the sixth grade that division became apparent, and racism flooded my everyday life. I was called everything in the book: *wetback, spic, border jumper.* When I mentioned this to my mother and neighbors, they told me the history of the Mexican culture. My culture. The short version is that our ancestors were deceived, killed, raped, and our land stolen. They call us *wetbacks* because Mexicans swam to get to America. Knowing all this, I was a bit confused. I was born in Phoenix, Arizona, in the United States of America, yet I was still being called derogatory names.

Over the years I became intrigued with my ancestry. I wanted to find out more, so I turned to books for answers. The more I read about the history of America and Mexico, the more I felt like there was something missing. I was twenty years old before I found out that every Mexican possesses an ancestral lineage to an indigenous history. My history was aligned with the Mexicatl/Aztec people. Now I was ready to learn about my culture, people, and traditions. At twenty-three I was introduced to Mexicatiahui, an Aztec Dance circle in Portland. Mexicatiahui means *moving forward*. This gave me the strength to move forward in every aspect of my life. The struggles of my present-day life seem minimal compared to the hardships of my ancestors. Because of this perspective, I don't quit, I don't give up, and I don't feel sorry for myself. I continue to learn from this cultural circle, and to be inspired by Aztec dances, theology, philosophy, songs, drums, and other traditional ceremonies. I named my children Nahuatl names so they will always live with their culture.

I now teach the dance of the Aztec. I also honor my culture with song and ceremony, as I honor my ancestors who fought to keep these components alive for us today. Aztec dance is only one aspect of the beautiful Aztec culture, yet it is the foundation for me to connect with my true identity. My personal belief is that our history is a key. Understanding our past, from childhood to adulthood, is an important component of being human. It connects us to our surroundings. For instance, my culture and tradition provides a strong respect for our mother earth, nature, and all creation. We can learn from past teachings that will better our future. Welcome the good with the bad. Shift the mindset of our children to embrace diversity and improve our environmental impact. Pioneer for the next generation. My true history was not written after the conquest of Tenochtitlan; it begins thousands of years before when the Spanish stepped foot on what, today, we call Mexico.

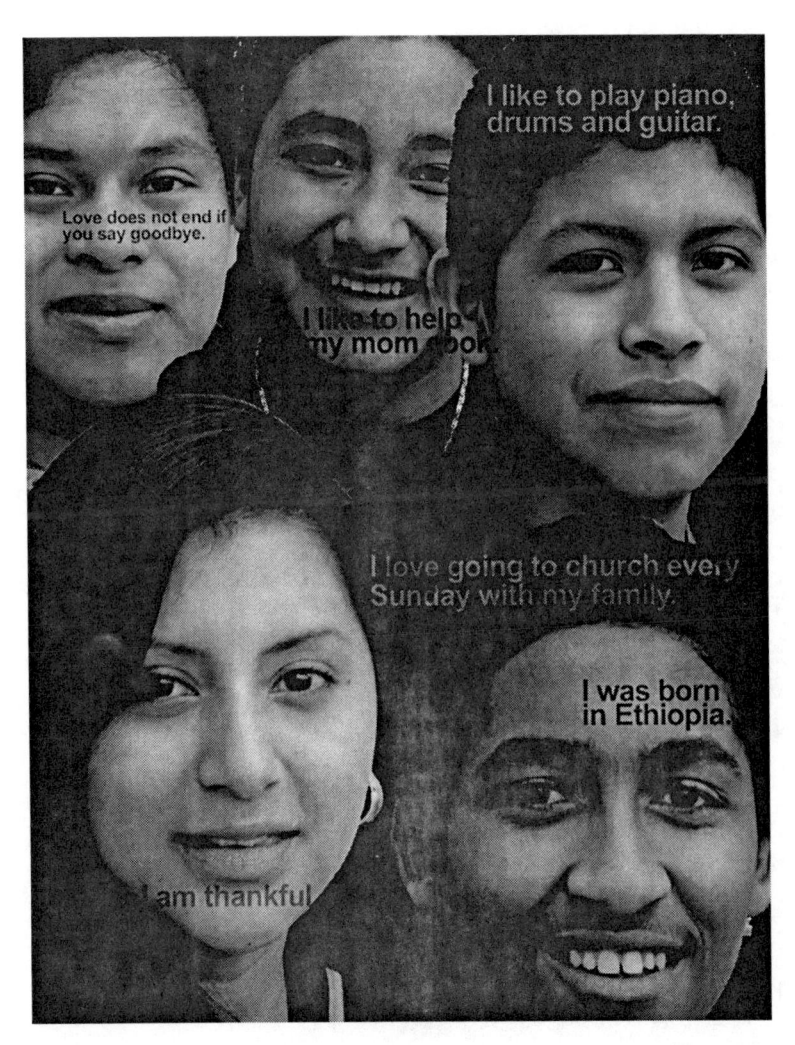

By Jeri Lee

Fly

Lucía Gaspar

We would like you to know
That we are not here to be despised
But with a purpose to fulfill
We are not all brown with dark hair
Our race runs through our veins.

Let me introduce to you Lucía
Who is of the butterflies and bunnies
Of tamales and empanadas
Of tortillas and coffee.

I would like you to know
That we don't depend on the government's money
But on our efforts and sweat
That not all of us walk around with a dry brain and without
    manners
That not all of us walk around in dusty clothes smelling of sweat.

Lucía
Who is of the field
Ball from foot to foot
From one side to the other
Goal…
Soccer…
The sport for most of Latinos.

I would like you to know
That not all of us are unemployed because we are lazy
But because of the rejection we endure for not knowing how to
    speak English
Because of the rejection we endure for being indigenous
And not being "equal" to them.

Lucía
The one with open wings to fly
And hands filled with difficulties

Who sees life like a mirror
Who smiles when you look at her smiling
The butterfly that wants to become a psychologist
Eyes shining with hope
Looking for closed doors to open
She holds the key in hope
Ignoring those voices that whisper *You can't.*

I would like you to know
That not all of us are from fights and gangs
Not all of us are from the same Latino language
Not all of us are illegal.

Lucía
With Chinese eyes and Guatemala roots
With long black hair floating like leaves in autumn
Although she is Chicana others define her as illegal.

I would like you to know
that we are all worth the same
That we work hard to raise our families.

We would like you to know
that we are proud to be who we are
That we are eagles looking from afar at a better future
With wings wide open and ready
To fly far away and reach our dreams.

Volar

Lucía Gaspar

la de las mariposas y conejos
la de tamales y empanadas
la de tortillas y café.

Me gustaría que supieran
que no dependemos de dinero del gobierno
sino de nuestros esfuerzos y sudor
que no todos andamos con el cerebro seco y sin buenos modales
que no todos andamos con el olor a sudor y las ropas empolvadas.

Lucia
la de la cancha
pelota de pie a pie
de un lado para otro
golazo...
Futbol...
el deporte de la mayoría de los latinos.
Me gustaría que supieran
que no todos andamos desempleados por flojos
sino por el rechazo hacia nosotros por no hablar inglés
por el rechazo de ser indígenas
y no ser "iguales" a ellos.

Lucia
la de alas abiertas para volar
con la mano llena de dificultades
pero ve la vida como el espejo
que te sonríe si la miras sonriendo
la mariposa que quiere convertirse en psicóloga
con los ojos brillando de ilusiones
buscando puertas cerradas para poder abrirlas
con la llave que sostiene en la esperanza
ignorando esas voces que susurran *no puedes*

Me gustaría que supieran
que no todos somos de peleas y de pandillas

que no todos somos del mismo idioma latino
que no todos somos ilegales.

Lucia
con ojos chinos pero de raíces de Guatemala
con el pelo largo y negro flotando como las hojas en otoño
que aun siendo chicana para otros es definida ilegal.

Me gustaría que supieran
que nosotros también valemos de la misma forma que los demás
que nosotros trabajamos duro para sacar adelante a nuestras
    familias.

Nos gustaría que supieran
que estamos orgullosos de ser lo que somos
que somos águilas mirando desde lejos hacia un futuro mejor
con las alas abiertas para volar lejos y alcanzar nuestros sueños

Just because I'm a cheerleader
I'm not always a happy camper
I am an emotional wreck
I have mood swings
The best thing I can do is fake a smile
Natalii Sriscointon

    Just because I wear black makeup
    Doesn't mean I'm a Goth or that I'm weird
    Amanda Cuthrap

        Just because I'm a teenager
        Doesn't mean I want to grow up
        Maggie Campbell

            I'm proud to be African, it's who I am.
            Dacha Kali

By Kierra Mathis

A Home in Two Countries

Espoir Mbirize

My life has been a difficult but rewarding journey. I was taught to learn, listen and respect in a different way from others. Before coming to the United States I lived in East Africa. A civil war in my family's original country, the Democratic Republic of the Congo (DRC), forced us to leave. We moved to Nyarugusu, a refugee camp in Tanzania, where we lived for ten and a half years.

We wanted to stay in our original country, but we had no choice. We left our father by himself in the Congo, suffering from being beaten all over his body. He looked at us like he was not feeling the beating he was being served, but suffering from the loneliness of being left by his family. I wanted to help him escape, but I was too young to do anything. I remember sitting in the boat, waving to our father while we were all crying and he was yelling to us that he wished he could be with us. My mother sat in the boat while her face looked very confused and I could only imagine her thinking about how she was going to raise us without our father when she was suffering from diabetes.

I wondered how we were going to survive without my father. I cried every time I thought about him. Daily life was a disaster because we were always sad. Our family was incomplete. When I was three and half I started to think of the responsibilities I would have when I grow up. I knew my mother was going to suffer even more from her stress of not being with her husband and raising us than from her diabetes. I knew she would suffer to find food for her children. I could tell all this by looking into her eyes. She didn't smile like she used to.

Life was a struggle for everyone; food, clothes and shoes were more than we could afford. Jobs were scarce and income was little for those who could find work. People had to recook the same food day after day so the camp basically smelled the same every day. Conditions weren't sanitary and many became fatally ill. Although I was very young, I was working as an adult and looking after my younger siblings. This was not easy for me. My mother was sick most of the time. She spent her days and months at the hospital.

After two months, which had felt like a year, my father joined us at Nyarugusu camp after surviving the beatings and the dangers he faced. He began to work for his family by cutting and selling firewood. Soon he got a job as a security guard at a Red Cross hospital, but he barely received enough money to feed the family. My older sister was the person we all depended on to cook and to do the chores. My job was to make sure my younger siblings were at home on time because they were not allowed to be outside after five or six in the evening. I was also responsible for getting enough water for drinking, cooking, and showering. I had to give my younger siblings showers, cook the food, and deliver it to my mother at the hospital. I did all this every morning before going to school.

Even though I was powerless to solve his struggles, one day I asked my father, my hero, if it was okay for me to help him with the responsibilities because I felt like he was overwhelmed every evening in the end of the day after work. He smiled while kneeling and told me, "You're an incredible and intelligent son. I hope that you'll always remember to serve others even in the most difficult moments." I'll never forget these words and the tears in his eyes despite his smile. I learned then how joy and pain come together. I cried and wished I could hear the wisdom my mother would share if she were there with us.

In addition to working hard every day, my father also made sure that we were doing well in school. He didn't want to pressure us, or our mother in the hospital, with more chores to do at home. They told us often that they wouldn't let anything interfere with our learning in school. So my father did them. I was often stressed because of my mother, who was now pregnant and no less ill. We didn't know if she would ever deliver her baby. I both admired and felt sorry for my father because he was a man who never stopped serving his family, no matter how many difficulties were piled on top of him.

My uncle was also an incredible person whom I spent a lot of time with when I was ten. I loved being around him because he had high expectations for my future. He taught me a lot about what to expect. "Life is a school," he said, "and obstacles are tests that you have to overcome in order to succeed." To me, these were the most beautiful words and last thing I heard from him.

When my mother was released from the hospital, she was called to the United Nations High Commissioner for Refugees (UNHCR). When she returned home, she told us that we might be moving to the United States because my little brother who couldn't walk, nor feed himself, needed special care. It was upsetting because we didn't want to leave our loved ones. On the other hand, we were so excited! My parents wanted my siblings and me to pursue a successful education once we arrived. We knew the way to make it happen would be to move to the West. We decided to celebrate instead of mourning the change, because leaving was an opportunity for a better life. We couldn't believe we were actually going to the United States, which we called "Earth-like Heaven." We thought that we would finally live without struggle and get to relax....

I was thirteen when I first stepped off the plane in New York. It was 2010. I immediately felt more freedom than I'd ever known, and pictured a great future for my family and myself. The floor in the hotel was shining like an untouched mirror. I went outside to see the view and it was the most beautiful place with tall buildings and wonderful trees. I felt like I was in a different world. I was. Everything I needed was there for me to reach. I felt safe as my family sat enjoying the view. America was truly the place to set our goals.

I began to taste different foods like rice, beans and chicken. I felt the support from different people who, like us, were from different countries. Here we all were, united in the same place. What most shocked me was seeing an old woman driving. I'd never seen a woman driving before in my entire life. I knew my sister was going to be a good driver and that she would teach me. I had a feeling that I would thrive.

However, there has been struggle for my family. Because my parents did not speak English, they found it difficult to get good jobs. I knew it was up to me to make sure I stayed focused in school, and learned English as quickly as possible. To others it seemed like I was too young to help my parents, but I went with them to the market and found jobs for them online. Learning a new language made it all possible. But I still needed parents. I depended on them like a leaf to a tree. My older sister was grown-up now and planning to get married. That meant I would have more responsibilities at home. I knew how much I would miss my sister when she moved out. I cried every time I thought of her because she was my closest friend.

America did not let us down. My family was thankful for the things we received from people in the neighborhood. America was the place where my mother was less sick and spent most of her time at home. America was the place where my father earned a good income, and could afford to buy us food and school supplies. America was the place where kids could learn in and out of the classroom. In the classroom, I studied hard, wanting to keep my parents happy and proud. Out of the classroom, I worked hard, wanting to keep my family together.

I know how it feels to suffer from pain and sickness. Now I know what it's like to feel accomplishment. I've been working hard to improve my English, to keep my grades as high as possible. One of my greatest desires is to help my family. I know they will struggle more than I do because they don't know how to speak or write English. As the oldest boy, I must take responsibility as a man of the house.

With daily help from my teachers, I've been able to identify my identity more deeply. My purpose in life is to serve those who need to be helped and encouraged. As a doctor I could assist those from different countries. Both of my parents and my uncles have encouraged me. Living in a new country is hard to adapt to, but with motivation and family support, I know I can succeed.

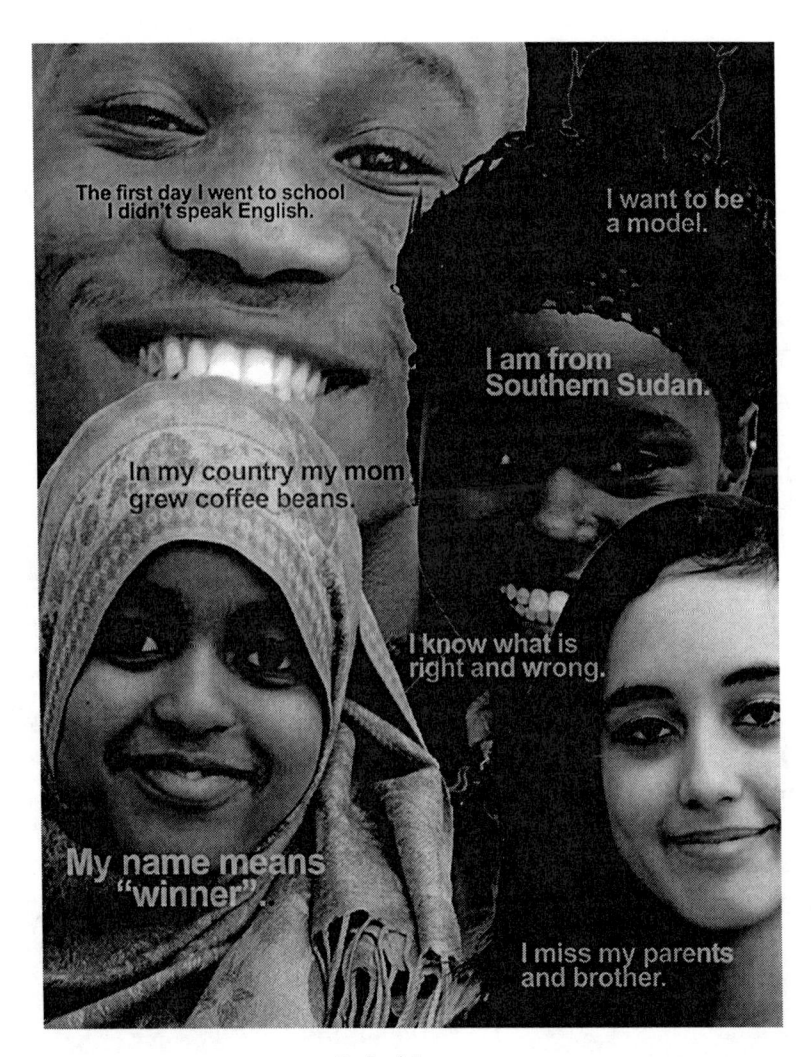

> The first day I went to school I didn't speak English.
>
> I want to be a model.
>
> I am from Southern Sudan.
>
> In my country my mom grew coffee beans.
>
> I know what is right and wrong.
>
> My name means "winner".
>
> I miss my parents and brother.

By Jeri Lee

Conversation

Doua Vang

This conversation could take place at school or anywhere...

Collin: What are you?

Mai: I'm not a what, I'm a who; I am Hmong.

Collin: What's Hmong?

Mai: Most Hmong people, like my parents, are from Laos or Thailand, but the Hmong are originally from China, living in the high mountains.

Collin: China? Laos? Thailand? How did you get here?

Mai: The CIA recruited the Hmong men in Laos to fight with them in the Vietnam War. Eventually, the Hmong and the Americans lost the war, and because of the defeat, they had to find a safer environment. Therefore, they migrated everywhere, like France, and Australia, but most of the Hmong people moved to the United States because *the Americans* were the people who recruited them and it was *their* responsibility and *they promised* to provide safety to the Hmong people.

   Way too many of my Hmong people had died after the defeat. A lot of Hmong families lived in refugee camps more than five years. During the time, no one could leave the camp and many people got sick, especially children.

Collin: How is living in America challenging?

Mai: Well, for one we don't have celebrations like American people do. The only celebrations I can think of are Hmong New Year and weddings. In the American culture, we have Christmas, Valentine's Day, Easter and so many more. Halloween must be the scariest day for many Hmong people who arrived in the United States because Hmong people have beliefs in the spirits. So on Halloween, when they open the door, they would see children and adults in their scariest Halloween costume, and they will mistake them as bad spirits or ghosts.

Collin: (laughing) Sorry, but that is just funny. I mean it's understandable, but sort of funny.

Mai: (laughing) Yeah, it is sort of funny. I just feel bad for those who experienced that. They must have had a small heart attack on that day.

Collin: I bet. How do some other differences about Hmong culture compare to the American culture?

Mai: Personally, I think the Hmong people are a lot different than the American culture. Like, we have a lot of traditional values: family structure, the language, healing ceremonies, and just so many more under these traditional values.

Collin: Tell me about it.

Mai: Well, family is probably the biggest one that the Hmong people value most because we can support each other. This can lead to having more children and to teach them the traditional customs. In the Hmong culture, we have about sixteen to eighteen clans or last names, like Cha, Yang, or Moua. These are just a few last names. As a Vang, I cannot date or marry anyone with the same last name as me, even if we are distant, we cannot date. Though, the funny thing is I can date whoever is on my mother's side of the family, a Xiong.

Collin: Woah! Wait; let me make this clear. So you can't *ever* marry anyone with the same last name?

Mai: Correct. I can't *ever* marry anyone with same last name as me, but I can marry anyone on my mother's side of the family. As a Hmong child, you have to take your father's last name. If I marry someone with the same last name, it will be disrespectful and dishonoring to my family. The reason why we have to marry someone outside our clan is to carry on our father's name and expand our family.

Another difference is health care. I am from a family who still follows the traditional Hmong spirituality. My family still practices shamanism, an act of healing, or communicating with the spirits. We would hold ceremonies for when a person is sick, and the shaman would communicate with the otherworld and to see why a person is sick. The healing ceremony takes up most of the day.

Collin: How does a shaman heal?

Mai: Good question. I don't know. *laughing* I guess, the way my uncle tried to explain to me was that shamanism is not a medication. Shamanism is a spiritual healing, which means the shaman's spirit communicates with the souls or spirits, which is why the healing will take up most of the day because the shaman's spirit does not go to just one place, but to many other places, to communicate with the spirits.

The family supports the shaman in many ways. For example, as the men in the families will help the shaman. Without the support from the family, the shaman would most likely not be able to do his rituals.

Collin: Interesting! How is your language unique?

Mailee: When using the Hmong language in a sentence, it is very similar to English. We follow the subject-verb-object structure, but there isn't exactly a verb tense so the listener has to listen carefully on the context of the sentence to identify the meaning.

Mai: When speaking, if you use the wrong tone, you are saying something totally different to what you want to say. It's very complex to explain and understand.

I grew up learning this, and it is still complicated for me to gather. Oh, do you want to come over next weekend to watch us do a ceremony at my house?

Collin: That would be wonderful! What kind of ceremony?

Mai: It's a blessing ceremony for my niece to call her soul home. We start early like at least 7AM, but we don't eat until like late afternoon, so you can come whenever.

Collin: I'll come early to watch you guys.

Mai: Sounds good then. I will see you later then

Collin: Okay. Bye Mai.

Masterpiece

Walidah Imarisha

When I die
I wear nothing but the tats on my back.
—Kakamia Jahad Imarisha, "The Last Stand"

His body
Tapestry
Memory
Masterpiece
Writing his name on the sun his skin
Roadmap of ink and flesh
Raised keloid scars
That can be read like Braille

My adopted brother
Kakamia Jahad Imarisha
I named him when I was 17
He was reborn under my breath
And you know what the elders say
If you name it,
It is yours

mouth full of broken angel wings
and arm full of India ink

Rage seeped in with that ink
Injected by a prison gun
Deposited just beneath the exterior
In bold styles
No one could ignore
Crept up his neck like ivy
Encased him in an armor of his own design

the cynicism of
fuck the world
spans his back
in bold old English letters
intersecting his hope

Afrikan warrior
Shield and spear in hand
Rises like the sphinx from the small of his back
Shadowed by a one-foot anarchy symbol
Thug scholar to ruffneck revolutionary
Machetero symbols
Kamikaze graffiti
And a fucked up picture of Da Brat from when he was 15

And no box can hold him

the doctors told him to lay off the toxins
when they cut out the cancer
that was located directly under his right nipple
there is a two inch scar
camouflaged by the Afrikan symbol for
eternal energy
he paints his scars brightly
in defiance of death
mocks the Grim Reaper
by taking his name
and painted a bulls eye in the middle
of his chest
with the edict *no warning shots*

His whole life has been a carcinogen

My brother is a living memorial
A walking Vietnam wall
A place people go
To remember atrocities
To mourn lost loved ones
To pray for forgiveness
To vow
Never

Again
Victoria
Jackie Jr.
Thearon
Dice
Qui-Que
A litany of those
Who slipped through fingers
Outstretched through bars
Dead partnas
And mommas
Sons
Brothers
Cousins
All on his body
They walk with him
He walks with the weight
Of exquisite corpses
His footsteps thump
Like thunder
And echo tenfold
For the multitudes
Who live
Under his skin

He carries a picture of me embedded over his heart
We breathe as one
His name soaked into my wrist
Pulsing with my pulse
We inject our familial bonds
Needle connecting us like an umbilical cord
Blood clots slightly around
Tender flesh
We are joined by more than blood and ink
We chose family

By Julie Keefe, Doua Vang, and Jeri Lee

Blended Culture

Nathan Buckland

It's Thanksgiving Day. You wake up to the sight of a cultural mixture of food. In the open air resides the aromas from fresh-out-the-oven turkey, honey glazed ham, and mashed potatoes. Your mouth waters at your imagination creating the possible flavors of the egg rolls, laab, and kapoon. With a kind greeting, your American father and Laotian mother ask you for assistance. Two cultures collide, greeting one another with open arms.

As you scramble around the kitchen, family members roll into the house constantly. Happy faces stroll in as more food of a cultural mix flows into the house. It is phenomenal. It's great to have a cultural background, but it's even more enriching to have a blend of two cultures to experience both sides.

It's important to have the ability to live as you please—doing what you will without having a cultural norm "disgrace" you or "shame" you and your family. But also at the same time, you respect your ethnic culture by abiding to it in the times where family is most important. The two balances together build stronger and tighter bonds between families.

Parents are closer to the children and understand their needs and respect their dreams. Children are happier and even the sight of it creates a soothing aura for the entire family. Families are stronger, happier and more connected to one another. With two different cultures, a child can reach out to either parent for different situations, further developing their knowledge as a whole. For the more ethnic and cultural questions, I go to my Laotian mother, whereas some of the more basic questions of modern culture I ask my American father.

Whether you are biracial or not, why not continue to build mutual happiness in families? Difference is what makes friendships. As cliché as it sounds, opposites attract. Diversity creates an environment that welcomes all. Acceptance is stronger than ignorance. Personally, it is better to adapt and grow into a new person than it is to repel and avoid new experiences and opportunities.

Mindset

With realization of one's own potential and self-confidence in one's ability, one can build a better world.

Dalai Lama

Your stay may not have a happy beginning, but that doesn't make you who you are. It's the rest of your stay where you've chosen to be.

The Soothsayer
Kung Fu Panda 2

Torn

Shandi Borchin

Angry at the chaotic world, and the ignorant people in it
Sad because it hurts, but it's never ending
You can say you know me, but do you really?
I'm the girl who hides her feelings
It's funny how you think you know me

Angry at myself, never worthy
You can push me down, but never hurt me
Words of hate and full of lies
I hide in the dark and close my eyes

I block out your face
Your words
Your hate
I try and smile, but it's always fake
You think I'm happy, full of joy
You think you know me, but I'm just a toy
You run my life, you pull my strings
What you want me to be just isn't me

Torn between hiding and being seen
Do I tell you who I am or just let it be?
If I open my mouth and let it out
My anger
My sadness
My stupid self
Will it make a difference or change a thing?
You say you know me, but that's a dream

I'd change for you, I'd make you happy,
But no matter what I do I'm never worthy
So in the dark I'll always stay
With anger and
Sadness locked away
Like a child I'll cry at night
I know you hear me, but that's alright
Ignore my sorrow, ignore my pain,
Just like you do any other day

Torn between hiding and being seen
Do I tell you who I am?
Or just let it be

Who am I?

Debra Mendoza

This is a question everyone asks themselves at some point
On the surface I am the happy mother of three
I am whole
I am complete
but if you scratch the surface,
If you look just a little deeper you will see
I am fractional and defective

I want to hibernate daily
I have been cut, stabbed and beaten
If I hadn't experienced so much I wouldn't be the substantial, self-sufficient woman I am

Who am I?
I am a survivor
I will never surrender just because life gets overwhelming
I will expose my own imperfections in the hope that others will know
they are not alone
If I help just one, I will be successful
I am my mother's daughter
I am my daughter's mother
I am alive and I love to live

By Anthony Sylvester

Still I Rise

Maya Angelou

You may write me down in history
With your bitter, twisted lies,
You may trod me in the very dirt
But still, like dust, I'll rise.
Does my sassiness upset you?
Why are you beset with gloom?
'Cause I walk like I've got oil wells
Pumping in my living room.
Just like moons and like suns,
With the certainty of tides,
Just like hopes springing high,
Still I'll rise.
Did you want to see me broken?
Bowed head and lowered eyes?
Shoulders falling down like teardrops.
Weakened by my soulful cries.
Does my haughtiness offend you?
Don't you take it awful hard
'Cause I laugh like I've got gold mines
Diggin' in my own back yard.
You may shoot me with your words,
You may cut me with your eyes,
You may kill me with your hatefulness,
But still, like air, I'll rise.

Does my sexiness upset you?
Does it come as a surprise
That I dance like I've got diamonds
At the meeting of my thighs?
Out of the huts of history's shame
I rise
Up from a past that's rooted in pain
I rise
I'm a black ocean, leaping and wide,
Welling and swelling I bear in the tide.
Leaving behind nights of terror and fear
I rise
Into a daybreak that's wondrously clear
I rise
Bringing the gifts that my ancestors gave,
I am the dream and the hope of the slave.
I rise
I rise
I rise.

Born Again

Isaac Kelly

When I say I want to succeed in life, it's not about money or prestige. It's about doing my part to prepare myself for tomorrow. I only get one shot at life, and taking full advantage of it means the world to me. When I put my mind to something, I won't stop until I've earned it. I haven't always had this perspective, but now there's no going back.

Constant conflict marked my childhood. There was drama from my mother and brother, sisters and occasionally my cat. Everyday I was reminded of all the negative aspects of my life, and all the tumult began to become too much to handle by myself. What made the situation worse was that I was still trying to figure out who I was deep inside. There was no father in the picture to aid me along life's journey, and my mother had little to teach me of the trials of becoming an adult. All I knew was that once I was eighteen, I had better have somewhere to go; at the time I had no desire to go to college.

In retrospect, the most monumental change in my life came from an application that at first seemed so trivial. Nine year olds tend to not consider all the implications their actions have on the future, or all the forces in motion when adults make decisions for their children. When my mother forced me to apply to the Big Brothers and Big Sisters program, I let my discontent be known. I wanted to play, not dawdle on some lame program application. All I knew was that by filling out the application, I would be paired with another person, a grownup, who was looking for an underling. Little did I know, my mother was trying to find a person who could lead me where she couldn't. She was trying to give me a role model. And all the while, she had to deal with me and my hostility towards her for forcing me to sign up for something she knew would determine whether or not I would become successful as an adult.

A man named Christian became my mentor from the Big Brothers and Big Sisters program. We met the summer before I started middle school and we still hang out to this day. Over the span of six years, I have learned a great deal from Christian. When I was around twelve years old, if you were to ask me what I was good at, I would have said nothing at all. That would have been a lie, whether I knew it or not, because I had a gift. I had a gift that does not come often to children born in the 'hood: Christian. My exposure to Christian gave me newfound understanding of my own potential. I could do something with my life. Anyone could do anything if they wanted it enough. But for years, I was just some kid with things on his mind. I was not "anyone." My grades were low and I didn't know the first thing about being successful. No one had taught me until then.

I started building my character during my last year of middle school so that I could become the kind of adult I had always dreamt of being. School had become something I actually cared about, and my grades improved too. In fact, I earned the "Eager Beaver" award in English class. Things were looking up, until the second half of the year. I began to not care about my character again. Skeletons were still in my closet. I had hurdles in my mind to overcome before I could put all my energy into improving my future.

It was not until the first day of ninth grade that I decided to take another shot at becoming a successful adult. My first period was Algebra. I distinctly remember this class because I had failed Algebra the year before, and it frightened the hell out of me that I had to retake it. So, I did every piece of work she gave me. When my report card came in the mail, my mother yelled my name. A million things ran through my mind, like why did she sound so angry? I had worked so hard to get good grades, and now I was in trouble. My mom's face was glued to the report card as she asked, "Want to see your grades?" I took the folded piece of paper, heart beating like crazy, and quickly scanned. I had gotten nothing but As. Everything suddenly made sense to me; all the hard work I'd put in really did pay off. I was enjoying the fruits of my labor.

It was the summer after my sophomore year in high school, my grades were as high as ever, and I was reminiscing about all the things I had gotten to do. I won an award for my academic achievement, travelled to Denver to sell books, and passed my AP English exam. Now I was in my summer program at Brown University, sitting in my dorm room until my next class. Things had finally started to progress; my process was working. I was no longer that troubled boy trying to find himself. I had begun to understand a little more about my personality. Just three years before, I was struggling to come to school. Now, I just couldn't believe I had done it. I managed to change who I was, with the help of Christian. Then, I set my goals even higher.

You may be wondering what my process was exactly. When you are serious about a goal, you do everything possible to get one step closer. I tailored every decision to fit the future I envisioned. I wanted to be a biological engineer, so I took many science classes.

Afterschool clubs were helped prepare me for activities I hoped to do in the future. Books I read were about things I wanted to experience. What I've learned is that we have to remain completely goal oriented. Be relentless in the pursuit of your goal. You can decide who you are.

Don't You Know Your Worth?

Ania Warren

To see you go through the same stuff,
it makes me hurt.

You deserve more than
    a cheater and a liar
    a man who would use you to get what he desires
    puts you down low when you need to be up higher
    cryin' all night 'cause your heart's once again stomped on
    callin' yourself stupid 'cause for your pain,
You are the only one to blame.

You fell for his tricks and his talk.
You thought he was the real deal
but he was a fake just a slitherin' snake looking for prey

and there you were—guards down ready
to love, get married, have babies
live happily ever after like your dream said

but instead
you got knocked up and he is nowhere to be
found.

You wish you were dead, layin' in your bed until a voice in yo' head whispered...

It's okay. You're gonna make it through these days.
Don't give up on yourself.
Life's just begun. Stay strong and hold on.
It's just the beginning; better days will come.

A lover is not what's vital at this moment. Not for *you*.
A man is not what *you* need to make *you* more *you*.
Do things that make *you* happy.
Work toward *your* dream.
Why shouldn't things be as good as they seem?

Stay hungry for success and God will bless you with the best.
You will know if he's right...
There'll be no need for you to guess.

I Look in the Mirror

Faith K. Lao

I look in the mirror and I see someone who is supposed to be me. Is this person the someone that everybody else sees?

I used to identify myself as Asian, only Asian. It was how my eyes were and how my skin was "yellow." Or was it simply because it was where I was put? From the day we're born we're labeled; female or male. Caucasian or other. We spend our whole lives looking for a place to belong.

Identity.

I used to identify myself as poor, because growing up I didn't get what kids in my class got on Christmas. No new shoes or new clothes. I was bullied in elementary school for wearing shoes from Goodwill. Who was I going to be? Who am I? POOR. It made sense to me.

On July 27, 2009, I lost the most special person in my life, my grandfather. He was an orphan who never saw a lot of money, but he was ALWAYS happy. It was then that I realized that you don't know what you are really made of, until you are broken and forced to pick up the pieces. See, I learned that I wasn't the clothes on my back, the shoes on my feet OR the names I was called. Rather, I was myself. Me! Whoever I wanted to be. God's creation. I am the mistakes I make and the good I give.

Let Me Introduce You

Silvia Salinas

Let me introduce you to Silvia
Born in Mexico City, in Atizapán de Zaragoza County
in 1997
Where people walk like busy bees
And time passes like shooting stars.

A Birdie that flew far away from her country
Following her species in search of a better home
Only this time it wasn't for just the season
Because resources are more abundant there.

She comes from a humble and considerable family
They've taught her to value and to fight
Through thick and thin.

It makes her sad to see others suffering
It gives her goose bumps to see how tears infect her
While her happiness disappears.

It makes her happy to see others full of joy
And to watch the eyes of a loved one glow.

Amusement parks move her
For the moment she forgets she is sixteen and lives
Like a child without a worry.

It makes her laugh to see all the funny things that a baby thinks of
    doing
And to see how the arrival of one life changes the lives of many.
It makes her angry not to understand the lessons of everyday life
And to listen how, like a broken record, they are repeated to her
There is no duty that we neglect more than the duty to be happy.

She is afraid to disappoint those who believe in her
And let the glass crash in the hands
Of those who never believed in her potential.

Whatever happens, she will know how to devour bad thoughts
That could destroy her dreams and sink her
She will celebrate every achievement allowing her thoughts to dance
While thinking about what she'll become tomorrow.

Les presento a Silvia
Silvia Salinas Santos

Les presento a Silvia
nacida en la cuidad de México, en el municipio de Atizapán de Zaragoza
en mil novecientos noventa y siete,
ambiente donde la gente anda como abejitas
y el tiempo pasa como una estrella fugaz.

Pajarillo que voló lejos de su país
siguiendo a su especie en busca de un hogar mejor
sólo que esta vez no fue por el tiempo de la temporada
sino porque los recursos son encontrados con más facilidad.
Viene de una familia humilde y apreciable
donde le han enseñado a valorar y luchar;
a las buenas y a las malas.

Le da tristeza ver a los demás sufrir...
le da escalofrío ver cómo las lágrimas la contagian
y su felicidad se desvanece.

Le hace feliz ver a los demás llenos de alegría
y ver como los ojos le brillan a un ser querido.

Le emocionan los parques de diversión...
momento que olvida que tiene diez y seis años y vive
como una niña sin preocupación.

Le da risa ver cada chistosada que a un bebé se le ocurre hacer,
y ver cómo la llegada de una vida cambia la vida de muchos.

Le da coraje no entender las moralejas de la vida cotidiana...
y escuchar como le repiten como un disco rallado
que no hay deber que descuidamos tanto como el deber der ser felices.

Le da miedo fallarle a los que creen en ella...
y que el vaso de vidrio se estrelle en las manos
de los que nunca creyeron en su capacidad.

Pase lo que pase, sabrá devorar los malos pensamientos
que podrían acabar con sus sueños y hundirla
Celebrará cada logro y dejará que sus pensamientos bailen
al pensar en lo que se puede convertir el día de mañana.

Disability

My advice to other disabled people would be, concentrate on things your disability doesn't prevent you doing well, and don't regret the things it interferes with. Don't be disabled in spirit, as well as physically.

Stephen Hawking

A troubled life beats having no life at all.

Richard M. Cohen,
Blindsided: Lifting a Life Above Illness: A Reluctant Memoir

Narrative

Travis Koski

Some people may wonder what kind of identity does a person have by having an intellectual disability? There are tons of ways I can answer this question. My name is Travis Koski, and I am a sixteen-year-old sophomore in high school. Yes, stay off the road; I do have a driver's license! Anyway my basic view on identity with a disability is that your true identity is only affected by how you see the disability.

Going way back, I was diagnosed with Asperger's syndrome when I was just two years old. I went to elementary school up until the fourth grade. In the fourth grade though, the staff mainly were the ones that just did not really understand how to deal with my specific condition. I wasn't really bullied that much though, maybe a bit at times, but it was just the lack of understanding. My parents knew that it was not good for me to be around that energy, so then I was homeschooled all the way till now. My Asperger's never really affects me at all; sometimes I notice it more than other times. It affected me more when I was younger, but still not that bad.

There was still a silver lining in the clouds once I was homeschooled. My mom told me about this program called Special Olympics for kids like me. This program got me involved in different sports year around. The ones that I am doing right now are: track and field, soccer, and downhill skiing. But besides the sports, Special Olympics taught me a lot about my social skills, and made me a way more confident person all around. I have been in the program for five years already and I am going to keep going until I can't walk anymore. That is how much the program means to me.

I was feeling so good about sports that I wanted to break away from Special Olympics and try for a hands-on, competitive, high school sports experience! I tried out for soccer at Century High School for my first H.S. sport. I'd only had two months (at most) experience from Special Olympics. The ball may have been its own creature when it touched my foot, but I didn't care, I knew I didn't have that much practice. I really enjoyed soccer. After that, I actually joined Century's track team. Oh boy, that was a huge step up in competition level compared to Special Olympics. We had to train really hard, or else, come to race day, we wouldn't make it out there, especially because I was an 800-meter and 1500-meter runner.

But, other than doing well in my events for track, I totally thrived on the team, athletically, and socially. I made a couple of friends and just had a blast! Me and my mom were talking one night about how I only have two years of high school left, so why not go for a hands-on, real high school experience? I thought about that for a little while, and then we came to a conclusion. So, I am officially doing my junior and senior years at Century High School!

Now as far as your true identity goes, the way it is determined is by how you see yourself as an individual. If I told myself that my Asperger's syndrome degrades me and makes me lower than everyone else, they would all be able to tell I was thinking that. But instead, I tell myself that even though I am a little different, I am capable of the same exact things as everyone else, and we are all in this together. No one is higher or lower. Because of me realizing that, I have accomplished tons and am confident enough to try public school again! One thing to always remember is look for the positive, no matter what obstacle stands in the way!

And Proud

Josh Howe

I am from lost memories
From times spent looking at the sky,
wondering who I am
I am from hard days trying to get through to sleep
I am from bullies teasing me making me stronger
I am from books, the one thing that kept me from sadness
I am from family supporting me through all the hardship
I am from Asperger.
It's who I am, autistic and proud
I am from life, for life is what keeps me going

To Be a Roughrider

Jonathan Alex Rogers

I am Jonathan Alex Rogers, and I am proud to graduate from Roosevelt, 2013.
I am different, I am special, I am alone.
I am determined, it is all I have ever known.
I am a defender, a voice for the medically fragile and outcast.
I am a Roughrider.
We are kind and respectful.
We define our ability.
We know our power.
We believe anyone can be a Rider Hall of Famer.
We tackle the hard problems with guts and honor.
WE NEVER, EVER GIVE UP.
Riders on the Rise.

My son J. Alex Rogers graduated from Roosevelt last week and wrote this piece as part of the graduation ceremony. My son was born with the central nervous system in his brain. He has no corpus callosum. His right and left hemispheres are not connected and operate separately from each other. Making it through public school has been a challenge. He is highly functional for his disability, but struggles with social interactions with peers and adults. Roosevelt was a wonderful experience for him. We ended the year on a positive note. The students and staff of Roosevelt have created a culture of inclusion, something that cannot be measured by a test or score. And yet, something that will carry on throughout the student's life.

—Julie Ann Rogers, Johnathan's mother

The Strong One:
A Conversation with Brenda L. Dailey

Amber T. May

In spring of 2013, a top Portland graphic designer in her fifties was diagnosed with corticobasal ganglionic degeneration, a rare neurological disease inhibiting movement and cognition. This was the result of several years of testing. In spring of 2014, she was rediagnosed with multiple symptom atrophy, a type of Parkinsonism. She is wheelchair-bound and has limited use of her left hand. Brenda has been told that decline is inevitable and she'll never walk again. Never taking anyone at his word when the word is *never*, she works daily with her team of therapists and friends to reanimate her nervous system.

Brenda: I've always been really meticulous in what I do. And I've always been busy. Now I feel like I'm locked in my body. I watch people go around and do things for me; it drives me crazy. I want to pull my hair out but I don't. I can't.

Amber: Was the onset of the condition sudden or gradual?

B: Gradual. I didn't just wake up one day and couldn't walk.

A: What's changed about you and what hasn't? Other than the obvious.

B: I always used to try and keep a positive attitude and now I need to more than ever. If anyone around me is negative, I just shut it out and ignore them. I can't look at the bad things about my disease—how much I've been mangled and crippled. I look at the things I've made strides in. What's the word I'm looking for?

A: Progress?

B: Progress. And I look at that every day and am thankful. One thing hasn't changed. I would always look in the mirror before I left my house. I mean, this sounds vain, but I still wanna be presentable.

Maybe I haven't seen anyone all day except for my caregiver and husband, but it's still important for me to be presentable. Is that vain? I mean, is that part of my self?

A: It's way more substantial than vanity. You're trying to maintain your sense of normalcy, which is part of your sense of self, and can help to keep you from declining.

B: I guess it does bring my life back to normal, wanting to look nice because I always did before.

A: What do you miss the most?

B: My freedom. And by that I mean coming and going when I want to. I did all the grocery shopping and personal shopping and got flowers for the nursery....

A: Do people treat you differently than they did before?

B: Yes. They say, *Oh how good you look, Brenda,* and they don't know really what to ask me or what to do for me. I think they're scared of me because I'm in a wheelchair. And my voice isn't strong anymore, I talk so slowly and quietly now. People are loud and they just talk over me. My daughter-in-law always listens to me and makes a point to tell everyone to let me finish. She shushes up everybody and says, "Brenda's talking...."

A: Beautiful. So were you louder before?

B: No, I was always the quiet one. But I was normal-quiet so people could actually hear me.

A: How much of your sense of identity depends on how *others* perceive you?

B: Um, a lot. I used to be important in my family, deciding and planning everything. And now I don't know what's up or what's going on. They don't always include me and it bothers me. I think they're afraid to even call and ask how I'm doing cuz they don't want to hear any bad reports.

A: They contact you less to protect themselves from what's happening to you?

B: Yeah. I was always the strong one. After my sister died, everyone went through me to check on what was going on with the family. And that part of me hasn't changed so why have they changed how they treat me?

A: How much of your identity depends on *your* perception of yourself?

B: My perception of myself isn't very good because I feel useless. But I know I'm strong inside.

A: Where do you think your daily endurance comes from?

B: When I was a teenager I walked in on my grandpa getting really mad at himself because he couldn't lift a hundred pounds over his head. The guy was eighty-five years old! I was like, "Grandpa!" My sister got cancer and a three-month death sentence when she was twenty. She lived to be thirty-five. If she could do it, I can do it. It's just the way we were brought up.

When I was first diagnosed, the doctor told me that my tendons would shrink and then I'd die. And if I had any discomfort to take a Tylenol. I remember thinking, *My God, are you crazy?!* I said, "I'm just gonna shrivel up and die?" And he said, "Well, we all do, don't we?" I am gonna prove that son of a bitch so wrong....

Gender and Sexuality

Gender is not only women and sexual orientation has multiple choices.

Gloria D. Gonsalves

Inside every man there is a potential woman and inside every woman resides a potential man.

John Maxwell Taylor,
Eros Ascending: The Life-Transforming Power of Sacred Sexuality

What is Tattooed on Me with Invisible Ink

Zoe Senner

I've got expectations tattooed
all over my body
by a relentless society
if I lifted my shirt I could show you the one that runs
right around my waist
I could show you the ones on my breasts
they come with a warning label
this chest must be sexualized at all times
I could show you the ink on my chest
it only runs skin deep
and all it says is:
flat-chested nothingness
followed by, P.S.
to clarify, that means that these breasts must be chastised,
because the only value they've got is sexual, and bigger is better here
    in the U.S.
I've got tattoos that tango across my ribs and collarbone that say,
fill me with water
I tried to tattoo *feminist* across my heart
but I accidentally put a target on my back, and the word, the slur,
FEMINAZI right across my forehead
I've had *victim* tattooed between my legs since the night I was born
    and society labeled me *woman* without asking my consent
I've got *fighter* in permanent ink between my shoulder blades
because a fighter is what you've got to learn to be to be a woman in
    this country
a fighter is what you've got to be if you're gonna be queer in this
    country
and I've got this tattoo that only has
two words

but it's in various places all over my body
and it's screamin' for attention 24/7
SHAVE ME!
shave me, shave me, shave me, shave me
and no one ever tells a fox to shave its fur
because it's an animal and I'm an animal
but I can't look like one and I can't act like one
because I was born with instruction manual tattoos across my toes
they warn me about the consequences
I will face
If I do anything with my body that doesn't conform to our male-dominated society
If I do anything except unquestioningly and obediently accept
the expectations, labels, and identities
tattooed on me
with invisible ink

The Box

Wesley Cady

Male.
Strong
Aggressive
Abrupt.
Female.
Submissive
Attractive
Weak.
These are societal "norms."
And you don't fit
inside
these boxes like the mail.
Pack
Ship
Send.
That's it,
the end.
When people don't understand
why you are
the way you are,
they try to put you in a box because.
In that box
You
Are
Simplified.
They create the illusion they understand you
and that's the problem.

The box.
Square
Brown
Dull
Is
Not
You.
You are multifaceted and interesting.
Be you because
it's all you ever were.
Break down the boxes.
Stop using stereotypes like UPS uses packing peanuts
so all objects fit into their standard box size.
Pop the "norms" like bubble wrap and
Just
Like
That.
You can see that the thing
in the box is nothing
but me.

Heels

Loretta Stinson

Sly taught me how to walk in skyscraper heels. He showed me the trick of double-sided tape for traction, positioned on the sole of the shoe under the ball of the foot.

"Head back, baby. Don't look down. Nothing down there but dirt. Eyes up. Lead with your hips. Pay attention to me now." Sly, with his Eartha Kitt purr and closet full of glam.

"Baby," he says to me, shaking his un-wigged shorn black head. "What *is* that little outfit you got on?"

Me, in my All Stars and denim, my only attempt at fashion a too-small turtleneck from the shelter's free box downtown.

"Girl, I ain't taking you nowhere till you change. And by the way," he says, "put on some makeup. You so white, you like a glass of milk." Sly, with his Diana Ross wigs and his mile-long legs.

"I don't have any makeup," I say, looking down at my shoes, his shoes really—shiny black Mary Jane's with six-inch heels. Too small for him, but Sly has an arsenal of shoes—over a hundred pairs neatly stacked in labeled boxes, here in his basement studio apartment in the Haight.

When he stands up and brushes by me, his white silk kimono swirls around him like foam on a North Beach cappuccino. He stomps down the hall, returning with a handful of clothes. He tosses them into my lap. "There. Change."

I pull off my shirt and shimmy out of my jeans. Step into a short black skirt and leather halter-top. With fringe.

I wait for him to get dressed—a two-hour minimum process just for a trip to Woolworth's makeup aisle. I lie back on the batik-covered futon, raising my legs in the air so I can see these impossible shoes on my feet. My legs are slim from so little food and so much walking up and down the hills of San Francisco. They are smooth because Sly made me shave them. "It's all about grooming," he said to me, as he handed me a pink Lady Bic the first night I crashed at his crib.

We emerge from the basement's twilight to the street above. Sly in a women's belted cream-colored raincoat over a sleek jade sheath, his wig a towering maroon bouffant wrapped with a silk floral scarf. He pauses and opens his handbag, checks his face in the golden compact, clicks it shut and takes my arm, steering me through the streets full of people. It is a misty day in late October.

I try to walk quietly in the heavy shoes. I try to keep up, on toes tilted forward, focusing on where I place the loud heels. I am walking the way I would if I were home in the pasture, with a harness, sneaking up on an unruly mare.

"What is wrong with you?" He stops abruptly and I almost fall, but he holds me by the elbow and steadies me.

"My shoes are so loud," I complain, looking up at his kohl-rimmed eyes. "Everyone will notice me."

"Heels are meant to be loud," he says. "They announce a queen's arrival. Perfume and heels tell people someone special is coming. Someone of importance."

We continue on our way. His voice a low growl as we walk. "Head up. Don't look down. Scan in front while you walk. That's better. *You* wear the heels, they don't wear you."

Men turn their heads as we pass, some stare. But in this city, Sly is unremarkable in drag and I am just a girl with long brown hair and a crooked smile.

"Walk like the Buddha," he tells me as we approach Woolworth's double door. "Be mindful."

I am Sly's dolly for the short time I stay with him. He likes to dress me up. Likes to paint my face and instruct me in the *how-tos* of glam. He likes that I don't know anything about makeup, shopping, "The Life."

Eventually, this city, with its boxed-in canyons of cement and steel, chews me up, spits me out. I am sent back to the sagebrush and naked song of wind in the high desert, the rustle of aspen near the Little Naches River. I leave the city when the weather shifts, hitchhiking north towards the place where home used to be.

Thirty years later, I strap on my own black Mary Jane's and head out to catch the bus to the school where I teach. I scan the street ahead of me, chin up, shoulders back, leading with my hips, mindful as I walk, the half-smile of Buddha on my face. The sound of heels on the street announce my arrival.

By Bovianna Somsanouk

My First Manifesto

Victoria Braun

I hear your accusations, see your disapproving eyes
Your whispers, they travel down and around these narrow halls of lies
You file in, take your place, and proclaim humanity,
We are the blessed creation of humanity...!
...But at what cost?
Does being human have to be proven?
I thought we were all children of God
Yet you say I can't love her; he can't love him; she can't love them—
Well I ask you, Whom do you love?
Is it an idol on a cross, claiming compassion? (I see none)
I don't judge you for your beliefs; don't judge me for mine.
If her eyes can calm my fears, if her smile can kiss away my tears
Who dares to say that is a sin?
And you say, *I didn't raise you this way.*
Well this isn't about you.
It's not your fault, it's not my fault, it's not *a* fault,
It is not a fault.
I see no sin in grasping love where love lies, love has no distinct place.
You find salvation in a building with tall ceilings, where chants echo like screaming ghosts, lost in the halls of faith.
I find salvation when her skin touches mine, when I lose myself to a force greater than my own mind.
I feel God.
You can call this temple unholy, you can call me a sinner, but I know it's not true and I won't let you condemn and nail me to a cross I didn't create.
That cross has no place in my heart, there is no room there for hate.
So I'll keep walking this path.
You can call me a heathen; I'd rather be a heathen that your god hates than a liar who deceives my own heart.

Mating Call of the Great Northern American Bisexual Homo Sapiens

Jocelyn Loyd

"I don't believe that if I came out as bisexual the world would change. But it's really important for people to be truthful about who they are and fight for equality. We need to help the world usher itself into the next phase," said actress Oliva Thirlby.

It took many years, several incidents, and way too many awkward moments before I was able to view my own sexuality, as well as the need for equality, in the same shimmering light.

It may have developed sooner, but it was sixth grade when I became conscious of my inexplicably close feelings for my best friend who was also a girl. I still enjoyed talking to boys and crushing on hunky Hollywood actor Johnny Depp, but when it came down to it, I really wanted to hold a girl's hand, too. Today, *alternative* sexualities are progressively more accepted than when we were in the classy darkness of the fifties.

Growing up, I spent a lot of time with my Filipino grandmother Aloja, who was a devoted Jehovah's Witness. Until I was fourteen, she constantly took her stress out around me, calling me fat and useless, saying that no man would ever want me. Many times I had to hold back my sassy tongue to keep from shouting, "Well, that's okay! I don't like them much, anyway." But from a young age I knew that she wouldn't understand, mostly because I didn't either, but also because we learned from the Bible that love and marriage is solely between a man and a woman.

Throughout middle school I felt confused, depressed, and upset. I wasn't like the other girls; I didn't giggle when a boy looked at me, nor did I write someone's name all over my math notebook with hearts and flowers. Though I did have a few friends who claimed to be bisexual, I couldn't confess; I would be mortified if I found out that they were doing it to be trendy. In the eighth grade I secretly confirmed that I was bisexual and there was nothing I could do about it. This revelation kept me out of the junior high dating scene.

High school was a bit better—at least I wasn't being called a fag anymore. Notably, I had my share of relationships with both genders, and I found more acceptance from peers who did not gawk when I told them of my identity crisis. There were only a handful of heart-breaking moments. From them I learned more about myself and my strengths as an individual of the LGBQT community.

During freshman year I did try to date a few guys, though the relationships turned out to be more atrocious than a cake baked without flour or eggs. It was also the year I received my first kiss from both genders. One was from a not-so-friendly friend who would, two semesters later, wound me with "Eww. Get away from me, you lesbian," because she wanted to look cool in front of a homophobic friend. She used the L word against me; it was an insult that took longer to heal than a physical injury.

When I first told my grandmother that I liked girls, we were in her car, driving home from a religious sermon. I do not remember what led to it, but I gave her my soul-baring confession and she did not handle it well. Later that day she told my mom, who in turn grabbed a few trash bags and filled them with all my books, CDs, and posters. To her, the media was to blame for my "sin."

"Mom, I like girls," I had said in my room.

"No you don't," she had insisted, not even looking at me.

"I'm serious. I've even kissed a few. I like it."

She left the room as if I was a disease, not her daughter. Even months later she was in denial.

I've faced my share of "Why do you like boys? Why do you like girls? What does marriage mean to you?" and it's never *not* awkward and uncomfortable. I used to always feel ashamed and as if I were sleazy, a source of entertainment. I am learning every time to take it with a grain of salt.

I am currently in a committed relationship with a brilliant and bright young man, but to me it's not a "heterosexual" romance. Sexual orientation is defined as "a person's sexual attraction toward members of the same, opposite, or both genders." He may be straight, but I feel like a tolerant and open individual. When people use labels it makes me feel as if my full identity is not being recognized or respected.

I once saw a movie that really made me come to terms with the fact that I cannot deny myself my true identity. *@SuicideRoom* is a very intense and emotional 2011 Polish film surrounding a nineteen-year-old boy, Dominik, who eventually commits suicide due to a depression derived from the brutal bullying he receives from classmates on Facebook for being gay. I connected with the confusion and hurt Dominik felt, especially when his parents openly denied that he was gay. I have also battled depression and suicidal tendencies, so seeing the way the characters reacted truly touched me. It didn't feel like a movie, I was left with the impression that I was a ghost haunting the tragic life of a misunderstood individual.

From my experiences I have gathered many truths. One, I cannot change the way I am any more than I can divert the direction of the wind. I am a creative, silly but responsible, gifted young adult— why change that? Two, the world may be advanced with its smart cars and super computers, but we are still many miles away from the finish line when it comes to equality. And finally, being openly bisexual or gay isn't an insult, but a victory.

To Inhabit the Body

Willa Schneberg

She tells me that as soon as those protrusions
sprouted, she knew they didn't belong.
They feel as alien, she says,
as the frilly pastel undies
her mother made her wear.
Grown-up, her body becomes her canvas.
She is sleeved-up with blue snakes coiling
her arms, their tongues darting out
underneath her chin.
She understands it is different for me,
that I don't want a permanent
testament to anyone inked in my skin,
and that when my chest was renamed breasts,
I welcomed those modest orbs.
She tells me that no one will ever talk at her tits again.
We both agree that is a perk, and that jerks
ogling me is my burden for liking mine;
and she will awaken from surgery
relieved that underneath her bandages
her chest is flat like a door
that opens into a garden
where she finds herself inhabiting
the body she was meant to wear.

About Me and You and Us

Amanda Saenz

A person is comprised of memories and experiences, and it's the culmination of these two that results in a unique individual. We are constantly changing and growing. Life presents us with new moments, each day unlike the one before it. Identity is fluid and dynamic; we are different today from the person we were a decade or a year ago. These changes can be at times imperceptible, but let me assure you, they happen.

When we reflect on who we are, some tenets remain concrete, integral parts of our character. Certain moments irreversibly affect our identities; their absence would result in a completely different individual. Yet, even with the existence of such moments, we can be almost instinctually drawn toward certain aspects and stimuli of this world. We find ourselves naturally passionate about only a handful of expression and actions offered. Identity, and the idea of "self," is then what drives our interactions with the world.

In my life various moments were pivotal in shaping the person that I am today. When I was thirteen years old, I was diagnosed as having an intersex condition. The term intersex is used to describe a multitude of genetic conditions that range from chromosomal variations of sex to ambiguous genitalia. As NPR reporter Sally Mauk puts it, an intersex condition is one where "genital or reproductive anatomy or chromosomal patterns are not clearly male or female."

My specific diagnosis is partial androgen insensitivity syndrome. This means that I have XY, or male, sex chromosomes, but I was born female in appearance. My body is largely unresponsive to the male hormone testosterone. Needless to say, this diagnosis greatly impacted my idea of self; it changed not only the perception of who I thought I was, but also my perception of other people. I understood the idea that those around me were more than they seemed on a much more intimate level.

My diagnosis mixed interestingly with my thirteen-year-old self's idea of identity: I was at the time in the process of accepting that I was a queer person. I held within me innate thoughts about who I thought I was, but had yet to fully acknowledge them, let alone put words to them. My diagnosis therefore acted as a catalyst for self-discovery. It made me confront my identity. It is therefore my belief that struggle can be a tool that allows an individual to learn more of themselves, their strengths, and at times their limits. Both my diagnosis and, subsequently, the sexuality that it helped me come to terms with complemented each other, the result of which allowed me to become proud of that aspect of my identity, which in turn allowed me to become proud of my whole self.

Today, I am an active member in both the intersex and LGBT+ communities, advocating for social justice and dialogue between the two minority groups.

Second, and perhaps the greatest catalyst in my journey of self-discovery, is college. A cliché, I know.

I had spent my formative years in a small town, attending a small Catholic school. I was unable to be open about aspects of who I was, and while I do not regret my time there, it was a bit stifling. Being away from this environment allowed me to be more myself and to learn exactly who that self was. While struggle can be a tool for self-discovery, so too can independence. I am not the person I was a year ago.

In order to fully realize what our identity is, we must first be in a safe environment that allows for exploration and discovery. College was a boon for me in this way.

My identity allows me to contribute to my world in a way that is totally unique; no one person is the same, and neither is their impact. Desire to change the world, whether it is their own personal world or the planet we live on, is intrinsically a part of someone's identity; we strive toward impact, toward remembrance.

My desire to effect change in my community is thus a direct result of who I am. I have had largely positive experiences that only propel and encourage me; adversity only leaves me with a passion to continue forward. For example, I do not blame anyone for being ignorant about intersex conditions. Instead of being affronted I choose to educate. I do not take ignorance personally. Intersexuality is a physical manifestation of a simple truth: that we are all different. We should not be defined, nor discriminated, based on our differences, but rather by our character.

Individual identity is a beauty often taken for granted, or rarely thought of. In the worst cases it is not even appreciated. But identity must be embraced, cherished, and most importantly, nurtured. The world we live in places a heavy emphasis on being normal. And while I can understand "normal" as a metric that seeks to identify the general mean, I cannot justify it as an ultimatum. If everyone were to abide by society's ideal of "normal," then we would all be the same. The result would be bland passivity, at the cost of colorful individuality.

That would not be a world that I would choose to inhabit; it is our differences, our respective identities, which make us beautiful.

Each day that passes we come closer and closer to understanding ourselves and seeing the beauty that lies innate within us. By recognizing and loving our own complexity, and by internalizing our own individuality, can we begin to see others in the same way. We are all on a journey to learn who we are and to discover our place in this world, a journey that will last a lifetime.

Relationships

I love you, and because I love you, I would sooner have you hate me for telling you the truth than adore me for telling you lies.

Pietro Aretino

It is not our purpose to become each other; it is to recognize each other, to learn to see the other and honor him for what he is.

Hermann Hesse

If You Leave

Emily Nowlin

If you leave,
who left will I have
to delight in
the silence between my heartbeats?
If you go,
which other will
appreciate
the truth in my jumbled words?

And if I stay here,
how will my song
ever reach
the skyline of a stranger's face?
If I still remain,
how can my smile
ever stand
to be thought beautiful again?

Because it's never enough to smile alone.

When you leave,
who more can I
feign to be
than shadows of the rainbow trailing from your soul?
So when you're gone,
promise to keep
my face
locked within your mirror.

For on that day
you depart from my side,
what else shall I
be to the world
other than a room without books?

Snowball

Troy May

as a young child i loved a kitten.
i loved a kitten desperately.
i thought she was a girl
because i was a girl.
i gave her a name
because I had a name.
i gave her a name to make her real
i named her
Snowball.
i loved Snowball with all my
fear, for my fear was fierce
and my love, desperate.
i thought
she was a girl who needed protection
because i was a girl who needed protection.
i thought
i could keep her safe
i thought I could keep her close
but i had named her and made her real
in a place where nothing
was safe.
as a young child
i loved a kitten,
i loved a kitten
named Snowball.
for one day
i held her.
for forty-five years I have mourned her

She
disappeared in the night
because i disappeared in the night.
as a snowman disappears
leaving his hat and pipe in a puddle
evidence that he was.
something fierce
devoured Snowball
because something fierce
devoured me.
something fierce,
without a name.
Something fierce without a name
devoured
everything.

Unwanted Born Life

Madison Parks

Through the soggy redness of teary eyes,
the past experiences of a life
The path of independence,
non-existent without guidance
Day to day on my own; now there are people
who think they can show me "the way"
Sleepless nights upon sad shades
of flashing lights, lids flicker
Thoughts remain
My head, a tornado
I shake all day,
no direction of where to go
If a state official isn't there,
nor my so called "mother,"
then who is?
25 say they are,
might as well be hallucinations
I drive myself tired playing,
"are they here or not?"

Poisonous Fantasies

Lara M. Carvin

Today you walked through the front door and I stopped short. You weren't sweaty from the hard day's work put in at the lumberyard. You weren't wearing a dirty maroon flannel shirt and workers' jeans. Your beard was expertly trimmed down. And to top it off, you had even come home early, foregoing a drink with the guys in favor of seeing me. As you stood in the doorway, dressed in an ill-fitting Oxford and wrinkly slacks, I couldn't fathom how this all happened.

    Later, when you offered to wash the dishes with a boyish smile, I felt repulsed. Who was this sharing my table? You took each plate and piece of silverware and began to wash them by hand. You wouldn't even surrender the task to the dishwasher. Using the rough side of the sponge, you carefully scrubbed away the stubborn sauce. Why hadn't you abruptly said thanks for the food and then retired to the den to watch Sports Center or that slutty reporter on channel ten? And then, after the dishes were all put away, you asked if I wanted a back rub. I almost walked out the door.

    When you finally drank a beer and watched the 49ers on Sunday. I sat by you, relieved. You ignored me and I could breathe. Then I saw that a light bulb was out in the corner lamp. Why hadn't you replaced it before I noticed? And the lawn… why wasn't it obsessed over? Why didn't you have lengthy chats with our neighbor Phil about what fertilizer works best? There was never an argument over flowerbeds or the damn weedwhacker acting up. Come to think of it, you didn't even seem that interested in the game. The Seahawks just scored again and you acted like it didn't even matter. Who are you?

You kept texting from the road saying how much you missed me. I rolled my eyes. Being on a trip with your dad and brother didn't make you forget to appreciate me. You kept saying that you loved me and that you wished I were there. Why can't you just go catch a fish, lie about its weight, drink too much whiskey and never call me, claiming no cell reception? My cell buzzed again—you included a wink smiley face. I turned off my phone.

    The flowers you brought home sat in a vase by the window. They were, of course, tulips. My favorite. As you cuddled up next to me on the couch I found that I couldn't stop staring at your hands. They were too soft and too clean—no motor oil or dirt underneath your nails. Where were the calluses? Where were your hardened muscles, earned by repeated swings of an ax? You kissed my cheek and handed me the remote. We can't fit together.

Today I left you. I moved away and put so much distance between us that there is no chance for following or turning back. Today I died. I had no choice, seeing as I had cut off my air supply. How can a person live so far removed from their sun, their air, their soul? But you let me come back to you. Of course you did. You live for me and I can't live without you.

Today I put on my plaid shirt, the one with the hole in the back, and replaced the radiator fan in your car. Then I sat on the porch with a glass of Jack, wondering if I should trim the hedges.

Family or Mami?

Diana Villalobos

Shadows only I can see

my mother's far, my family's here,
they surround me
as the clouds surround the sun.

A place the sun doesn't shine much
or a place the night comes faster
than you imagine...

Why must I choose?

How can I?
I need both:
the comfort of my family's land and
the magic of my mother's.

In my head, I hear their voices,
"Si te vas lo lamentaras."–If you leave you'll regret it.

Day and night the walls say,
"Hija te nesecito."–I need you my love.

The voices of my friends,
"What about us?!"

And,
"You'll find new friends, better friends."

I must choose between opportunities:
An education, a career, a secure life.

Or

happiness

(being by my mother's side).

Two things can complete my happiness.
It makes me wish there were two of me,
Why must I choose?

Dream, shout, cry
Shout, dream, cry
Sing.

Blame it on a secure future.
Blame it on wanting happiness.
Hard to have,
easy to desire.

I want
I need
Both.

Sisters' Sonnet

Rachel Pass

Two
Blood moved between our bodies,
    two fruits growing
    from a wishbone branch.
When I crashed my bike
and skinned my belly,
scaled silver paint flakes
from bike's stiff body,
its front wheel thrashing
like a salmon stranded,
you saw a picture in your head
of me, my gravel studded wounds,
and came running. You found me half
a mile from the house and used your strength
to limp me home.

One and One
Years later, I caught your image
in a net of dream and woke.
My muscles felt like apples pitted deep with bruises.
                      You told your story:
                car crash, whiplash, you promised
                      me you'd *be okay*.
    My blood and I believed that lie,
not suspecting
    that our branch's base   had cracked.
    My blood beat painless
        while his fists bruised blossoms
            on your skin.
                While his words seeded poison-rooted plants,
my mind stayed clear.

Couplet
I'd give my skin to hook us up again,
to graft another branch to hold us
        side by side   and pain to pain.
                I'd take it in; small price to know
                      you wouldn't hurt alone.

A Letter to My Adoptive Mother

Ellen Brahe

Looking back through old photos and a plethora of memories, it is now almost difficult, painful even, to reminisce on the process of my adoptive childhood. I obviously remember little, if any, of my actual adoption.

I remember only bits and pieces of my youth—you can recall more than I—but I do recollect one primal emotion throughout: Anger. I often distanced myself from you and from Dad because I was vexed at Jennifer, my birth mother. I felt she had abandoned me, and from the time that it actually mattered (namely throughout middle and high school), I could only bear to summon indignation; allowing the despair to take over would be too much for me to handle. I remember I often locked myself away in my room for hours on end, just to be away from the world and the feelings it let in.

Eventually, I began to funnel my anger and pain into a search of who I really was. People often asked what ethnicity I was, and when I couldn't properly answer, I was wrought with an insatiable hunger to find my true identity—a people I could feel at home with. What I didn't, or couldn't, understand at the time was that I had been given this from the beginning. People were so convinced we weren't family (I was infrequently asked why we weren't the same color) that I had started to believe it myself, and thus I lost sight of my people: You and Dad.

All you wanted was for me to feel at home, to feel happy in a sense of belonging. You helped me journey through a series of religious and spiritual cultures. We travelled together, as a family, and I found I often felt a greater sense of fellowship in the various countries we visited rather than at home. I rarely wanted to return to the States, so enchanted and satisfied was I with the semi-nomadic lifestyle.

Time passed and I reached the age when I was ready to leave home and go to college, seek a place of my own. It was only then that I realized how much I missed you both and how much I had always been loved. My desire to "get away" began to dissipate and was replaced by a need to return emotionally to my parents. I then made it clear I wanted us to be more than a mother and daughter—I wanted you to be my best friend, and I wanted to be your ally. And the way

you opened your heart so readily to me, to know you had been waiting so long for this was overwhelming.
    Finally, I am home.

Seeing Things

Cindy Williams Gutiérrez

It's just Mama and me. We live in my grandmother's old, creaky house on St. Francis Street, pretty close to the railroad tracks and church. I'll be starting school soon, but now I stay with the neighbors while Mama works. She's a seamstress and around Christmastime, for a little extra money, she irons other people's clothes.

After she finishes ironing each basket of clothes, she puts her nose to the men's shirts, the ones that are uniforms, and smiles, "Mmm, don't these smell good?" Sometimes she holds the shirts like she's hugging them. She says she loves making clothes feel warm and crisp. I love warm and crisp *buñuelos*—those big flour tortillas she fries and sweetens on New Year's Eve. Sometimes I wonder if she means that starched policeman shirts and sheriff uniforms smell that good.

It's a spring day, the color of heaven. My favorite blue—*celeste*. I just turned seven and we're on our way to Johnny's Ice Cream Parlor to celebrate.

"What do you see, *mijita*? In that one, the one with the puffy cheeks—see over there?"

She points to a slice of sky. "There, where it's all puffy and gray, and next to it is a long white streamer—like for decorating parties."

"An elephant. I see an elephant with an Easter bonnet on its head!"

Mama calls them cloud pictures.

"Exactly. I see your elephant too, Muñe!"

Muñe isn't my real name. It's short for *muñeca*—this means "doll" in Spanish. I guess you could say it's Mama's pet name for me. I like it much better than my real name, Mercedes. So when people ask, I just say my name is Mercy.

At the ice cream parlor, I order a chocolate sundae with lots of whipped cream and an extra cherry on top. I eat slowly, waiting for Mama to see faces in my whipped cream, maybe Santa Claus or Popo—Mama says he was round and jolly like Santa. I don't remember Mama's Papa much, except that his whiskers were white and tickly.

I like to watch Mama when she sees faces, like in clouds or in her bubble bath. Sometimes I peek in the bathroom door and hear her talking to the bubbles, maybe even crying or praying real hard, mouthing names. The names seem to go with the faces—these floating faces that sooner or later pop. Daddy's especially: Toño, his name over and over, rising up from her mouth like a bubble getting bigger and bigger—like it's just about to float away. Then her lips stop moving, she closes her eyes, swallows a bubble, and slowly dips her head under water. I was scared at first, but she says it's just like Baptism. Washed pure. And it doesn't happen often because she saves up her bubble bath for certain saints' days—I can't remember which, maybe it's Jude, the Saint of Lost Causes. Certain saints think it's very, very important to be impossibly clean.

At the counter, Mama only orders a Coke, but she takes a spoonful of my sundae when I offer. "Mmm, it's so delicious, isn't it?" I nod so hard Mama says my Hershey-colored bangs jiggle against my forehead. When I look up, I see Johnny, the owner, smiling big as a jack-o-lantern at Mama.

"Hi there, how about something else? You're not eating much today, Alma."

"No, thanks. We're fine." Mama gives him her dimpled smile—the prettiest one she saves just for family and close friends. Johnny fought in the Gulf with my Papi and Uncle Miguel. Not the Gulf we live close to, the Gulf of Mexico. This was some other Gulf far, far away on the other side of the world. After Papi and Uncle Miguel's funerals, Mama stopped going to the beach. She said sand, the way it slides so fast through your fingers—even when you scrunch it real tight, reminds her of that other gulf.

"Yesterday was my birthday!" I sing-song to Johnny.

"Is that so? Did you know we do special things for birthday girls?" From behind his back, Johnny produces a cloud of pink balloons tied with silver ribbon and a sparkly silver crown he places, carefully, on my head. "For you, *Princesa*."

"Oh! Thank you so, so much!" I jump up, try to wrap my small arms around the pretty balloon bouquet and Johnny, all at the same time. My crown spills off my head and my sundae tumbles onto the table—everything at the same time. All I can do is clamp my hands to my mouth, look at Mama, then at Johnny, then back to Mama. At the very same moment, we throw back our heads and all three giggle till it hurts.

Sometimes, on nights when I feel dreamy, Mama and I sit out on the porch swing and watch the stars. She says the glittery darkness rests her eyes. On this night, I dream of Homecoming, the sparkle of romance, of how I will glance at my very first date. Next Friday feels like farther than the farthest star. Tonight I rest my head on Mama's lap and let her stroke my long dark hair. She talks to me like when I was a little girl.

"Can you still see the two brothers in the face of the moon? The mean one, dark with envy, and the good one shining bright?" I don't answer, but keep looking at the velvet sky. We sit in silence, Mama wrapped in her white *rebozo*, like a gift waiting to be opened. I begin to see the ugly brother, his pimply-crater face, that gold-toothed grin like a lunatic. He's like crazy old Mr. Benavides who staggers down First Street arguing with himself. It's not so easy to focus on the good brother, his light almost blinds me. So I close my eyes instead. I can still see the stars shine in the familiar darkness where I make wishes. I ask each star to carry one of my secret dreams in its twinkling arms. The look in Tito's eyes, when he sees me in the emerald-green dress Mama made for me. The ribbons on the corsage of pink roses—curled like my hair when I wear it up. Our first dance, hardly breathing. And the goodnight kiss, the feel of it forever and ever and ever. I look up at the real sky and wonder if there are enough stars to light up all girls' dreams.

Sooner than I would like, Mama unwraps our gift, this sweet, dark silence. Her mouth presses to my ear. "God's sweet mercy," she whispers. "That's what you are, *mija*. God's sweet mercy."

"Tell me again, Mama, where my name comes from." I never get tired of some of Mama's stories—the ones that get better with each telling.

Quietly Mama takes a breath and holds it a minute before she speaks. "Sure, but just for you, Muñe." Mama smiles at me, then looks out at the black sky. "It was his last letter."

I quickly fill in her next pause. "The last one you received from Papi."

"Yes. You were just about to be born and he wished more than anything that he could be here. But he couldn't get leave."

"From the war. From Desert Storm."

"That's right. He was a soldier, that's what he did." Mama takes my hand, squeezes it tight as her eyes.

"So what was in the letter?"

"Hm? He, uh..." She clears her throat and goes on. "He said...he'd been thinking about you every day. That he'd even begun to hum a little tune he was writing for you."

"Papi had a nice voice, didn't he?"

"Oh yes, *mija*, he had a beautiful voice." Mama takes a long strand of her hair and curls it around her finger. "He used to serenade me all the time. It was the first sound I woke to every morning and the last thing I heard every night. He even waited till I finished my prayers to sing me a *bolero*. So I could dream of love, he said. He would sing me a love song before I went to sleep."

"How romantic, Mama!" I feel my pulse quicken, my cheeks color. I don't remember feeling this way the last time I heard the story.

"Yes, he was a wonderful husband." She sweeps the hair from my face and continues to lightly stroke it. "And he would have been a wonderful father."

"So the song, Mama, what was it? The one he wrote for me?"

"It's a love song, too, but more of a ballad. I think it was the only way…the way he could cope…with what was going on at the time. Let me see if I remember how it goes…the words are something like…"

"No, Mama. Sing it."

"But, Muñe, I don't know the melody. All these years I've tried to imagine it, but I don't know…"

"Please, Mama, try." I sit up and look straight into her eyes. "Try to imagine how Papi would sing the words he wrote just for me."

Mama smiles, closes her eyes, and begins to hum quietly.

> *Gentle singer, keep on singing,*
> *Gentle singer, sing the song*
> *That keeps me hanging on*
> *Till I'm back where I belong.*
> *Tender singer, keep on singing*
> *Tender singer, sing me a new life*
> *Where I can lay beside my wife.*

I rest my head again on Mama's lap. This is the part I like best, the part I've been waiting for.

> *Merciful singer, keep on singing*
> *Merciful singer, sing about babes*
> *The little soul my lone soul craves*
> *The soul whose mercies keep me safe.*

I let out my breath, feel the rush that comes from learning family secrets. The secrets of a father, and a name. I look up just in time to see a falling star brightening the night sky.

We're in Dillard's, shopping for clothes. Usually Mama sews most of my clothes, but this is a special occasion. Tomorrow is my first day of college.

Mama adjusts her bifocals, then takes a better look. "Muñe, doesn't she look like Perla?"

"Which Perla?" I try to whisper toward Mom and nonchalantly

eye the confident, tall, dark woman searching the sale rack across from us. Though I'd rather nonchalantly change the subject.

"Your cousin, the one that's studying at the Tech in Monterrey. What's she studying again? Agriculture?"

I'm not going away to school. A few years ago, our very own "tamale tech"—that's what we call the local junior college—became an extension to a major state university. So, I'll keep working at Barnes and Noble and keep Mama company. "It's called Agronomy, Mom. How would I know what Perla looks like now? I haven't seen her since I was fourteen." I groan, loud enough for her to hear.

But I take notice when I see the woman's honey-brown eyes are definitely a match to my cousin's. And her boyish haircut would probably look good on Perla. Never mind that this woman is almost six feet tall and doesn't have a single laugh line. I don't remember much about our visit to Monterrey that summer, but I distinctly remember immediately taking to Perla. For three reasons: she was puny, myopic, and a riot. "Well, I guess, Mom...sort of."

"What do you mean? They look exactly alike. Ay, que Perlita. I hope she's doing well in school. She's never really had a green thumb. Oh, look at this cute skirt, Muñe. Doesn't your friend Lydia have one just like it? The pleats, that lovely cinnamon color."

Lydia had lent me the skirt for a graduation party. Her skirt was more of a coffee color and the pleats were only one-finger's width. These were two-fingers wide, but I guess it depends who's doing the measuring. King Kong? "Um, I'm not sure. Maybe."

Sometimes I help Mama sew my clothes and help out with her orders. I don't work magic with a needle and thread—not the way she does, but I can handle most alterations. I'd rather save my eyes for books. I read all the classics I can get my hands on.

"Let me buy it for you, Muñe. It's so becoming on you." She holds it against my size 6 hips and smiles with pride, "You're such a beautiful girl, Mercedes, such a good girl." The edge of her mascara threatens to run.

"No, Mom, it's too expensive. Let's pick something off the other rack."

"No-no-no! You need something special for your first day of school. It's settled." She clears her throat and continues, a bit unsure, "It's so exciting...isn't it? It's OK to be nervous. Are you? Just a little bit?"

I look away, toward the store entrance. The stainless steel and glass doors morph into a portal of ancient marble. Athens, Rome. A passage to a world as old as thought. I feel breathless, as if I have run for miles to arrive at this very spot. This opening to a world of

108 – Relationships

unread books and strange ideas and unfamiliar names. A world that will open to me as easily as a new day.

And a world utterly foreign to Mama. My new life is a place she can't begin to pronounce. Like an alphabet that looks more like pictographs than letters. It is a strange place where Mama can't enter. She will try to hover, at its edges. But it will remain closed to her—like Texas rosebuds surprised by a sudden frost.

My heart thaws a little. I return her smile. "Sure, Mom, let's take it. Thanks." We walk arm in arm to the cashier, her face brighter than the store's fluorescents.

On the drive home, she points out a red Ford pickup that looks like Johnny's from the ice cream parlor. Same color, different make. He drives a Chevy. I gaze in the rearview mirror, at the shifting license plates of cars changing lanes behind us. I wonder what it's like to see glints of familiarity everywhere. The asphalt rolls by, monotonous.

"Hi, mija! How are you doing? Are you busy?"

Even as a starving graduate student, there are times I regret not spending the extra money on caller ID. "Hi, Mom. Well, I'm studying for my Orals. They're next week."

"I'm so proud of you, Muñe. You're going to be a doctor, a real doctor!"

"Well, at least in Greek philosophy and myth. What's going on with you? Is everything ok?"

"Oh, yes. I'm fine. I just thought I'd see if you were alright. I saw on the weather channel that it's twenty degrees in Boston—with the chill factor. Are you staying warm? Are you wearing the long underwear I sent you?"

I shake my head and nod all at the same time. "Yes, yes, I'm fine. I'm inside studying, so there's no chill factor in my apartment. Is that the only reason you called? Because I'm fine, really, I just need to study. This is my final requirement for graduation. So ..."

"Of course, mija. I don't want to take your time. It's just that ..."

"Just what, Mom? What is it?" Reluctantly I close my book, shift my focus from Daedalus to the waxy silence on the other side of the phone. "It's ok, Mom. You can tell me. It's time for me to take a little break anyway."

"No, it's nothing, really. I just got back from church and started cleaning out closets to donate some clothes. You remember the St. Vincent de Paul Society? They're such good people...they always make sure poor people have sweaters and coats and blankets in the winter."

I settle into the relative comfort of my fraying easy chair, rest my legs on the stained coffee table. I take a long sip of my *manzanilla* tea, the most important part of my ritual—the calming part—in preparation for long conversations.

"How could I forget? It's only been a few years since I stopped practicing. Thanks to you, I've been a Catholic twice as long as I've been a heathen."

"Sshh! Don't say that, Mercedes!"

"Why? Are you afraid I'll be struck down by lightning?" I'm barely able to contain a chuckle.

"I'm...I'm...never mind."

"No, tell me. I want to know." I resist the temptation to fill the long pause.

Then, as if letting out her breath in a phrase of soft song: "I'm afraid you've lost your faith, Mercedes. And without faith, you can't make it through this life."

Something in Mama's voice stops me short. It is as if the she has held the notes too long.

"Let's not argue, Muñe. I really called because I came across some of your things. They reminded me of when you were going to school."

I laugh. "Mom, I'm *still* going to school."

"Yes, I know, but when you were going to school *here*, you know, when you lived *here*, with me."

There is a stridency in her voice that unnerves me. "Sure, I know what you mean. I was just kidding. So tell me, what treasures did you unearth?"

"Well, remember that skirt I bought for your first day of college?"

"Uh, yeah...Of course I remember." Silence as I gulp my tea. "It's the pleated one. The color of brown sugar."

"Cinnamon. The one that looks so nice against your skin."

"Right. Cinnamon."

I wait for what sounds like static on the line to pass, then reconsider. "Mom, are you alright? Are you...feeling a little nostalgic? How are things with you and Johnny?"

"No. No, I'm fine. Perfectly fine. And you know perfectly well that Johnny and I are just friends."

"Call it what you want, but you've been inseparable ever since I left home. You can't fool me: you love taking care of him."

"You worry too much." Then clearing her throat, "I'm sure he's alright."

"What do you mean you're sure? When was the last time you saw him?"

"Mercedes, I didn't call to discuss Johnny. I just thought you'd like to know."

"Know what?"

"That you forgot your pretty brown skirt here, and that I'm saving it for you. The next time you come visit, you can take it with you—if you want."

"Sure, sure. I'll do that. Thanks for telling me."

"You're welcome, *mija*."

There's a break in the conversation, then I hear the static again. "Mama, is there anything else you want to tell me?"

"No, no. Just that. I better let you go. You need your rest before you take your exams. Get plenty of sleep and stay warm, okay?"

"Sure, Mom, I will." I hang up, uneasy with what Mama doesn't say. She doesn't say she just returned from a visit with the ophthalmologist. She doesn't mention glaucoma and macular degeneration. She doesn't say a thing about her sudden break-up with Johnny. She doesn't breathe a word until after graduation.

But I know even before she explains. I know because she comes to graduation alone. And because throughout graduation weekend, she doesn't recognize any relatives in the faces of my friends and faculty. She doesn't point out familiar flowers or furniture as we tour the Boston Common and Faneuil Hall. She doesn't even glance at the hazy sky over the Charles River.

Back home, even with the progression of her glaucoma and the return of her cataracts, Mama routinely recognizes her God and saints. She clearly sees their faces and reads their stories in church windows, on dashboards, even on trees. Like the ash tree in the front yard that still watches over her like an aging sentinel. On the few days it rains, this faithful ash collects raindrops in its canopy of leaves. Somewhere in its trunk, a patch of bark—about the size of the crucifix above Mama's bed—remains dry, gleaming white. But on rare, nebulous days when rain manages to crease this spot with moisture, this piece of bark becomes a shrine. It begins to varnish with epiphanies. Unmistakable traces of benevolent visages and folds of robes. At least in Mama's eyes.

Today is one of those days, a day when the sky is bayoneted with gray and Mama confines herself to her bed. She stares, unblinking, at her curtains. Her lips twitch like a nervous bird, still unaccustomed to, unable to shape the syllables of loss.

"Hi, Mama. I've come to see you. Don't you want to get up?"

I am a stranger to her. Boston is too far to fly down more than twice a year, especially for a full-time professor. I reach for her hand. It is as heavy and unfamiliar as the *manta* she once used to make peasant blouses. Only less durable, and not at all common.

"Come with me, Mama. I have something to show you. It's a surprise, just for you, Mama."

I squeeze her hand and will her to recognize the feel of my skin, my pulse and its erratic winged flight. To hold ajar the door to our history with this small fluttering gesture.

She sits up and I wrap her, carefully, in her old white *rebozo*–despite its imminent threat to unravel. She shuffles behind me to the front door. I reach back and take her arm in mine.

"Slow," she mutters. "I can't see well." Her cloudy gaze never leaves the floor.

We step through the door, stand side by side on the porch. Her body feels limp and frail, light enough for the breeze off the coast to toss her about like a small sailboat. I grip her arm tighter. She sags against me.

Finally, she looks up. The moment she lays eyes on the tree, something charges the air, a kind of lightning. Her head lifts and shoulders straighten. Two trembling hands form an immaculate steeple at her heart. Quietly she speaks of cathedral spires where branches soar. Her eyes brighten, focus steadily on the tree. Then a sharp intake of breath, and she clasps her hand to her mouth.

Suddenly Mama points at the bark, points and points at the sacred stain in the center of the ash, this unexpected dampness in the tree's womb. "¡Jesucristo! It's Jesus, *mija*, stretching His arms wide! There, Muñe. Do you see Him?"

I gaze at the spot, try desperately to discern something holy. If it were only a laurel...if only I could dig up this tree and point to its leggy roots. I could show Mama how the roots of her tree curl around the feet of Daphne.

Instead I search for evidence of nails. I look for rust-colored knots that could transform tree limbs into the arms of a crucified god. Then I speak in an even voice. "Yes, Mama, I see him. Of course I see him. The rain washed him clean on our tree."

She looks at me, begins to speak, but her voice catches. Mama closes her eyes, raises her arms to the sky. Her white *rebozo* falls to the ground.

"Here, Mama, you'll get cold. Let me put this on you." I wrap the shawl around her outstretched arms. Fraying, the long fringe flutters like feathers. She does not move. Then the long release of a cry, harsh and guttural.

I stagger backward, turn to see where this animal sound could have come from. The air is still, clear. When I look back at Mama, she is smiling at the sky, her white *rebozo* in full plumage. Two wings unfurl, aim straight for the clouds.

Race

I have a dream that my four little children will one day live in a nation where they will not be judged by the color of their skin but by the content of their character.

Martin Luther King Jr.

Our true nationality is mankind.

H.G. Wells

Bill of Rights for People of Mixed Heritage

Maria P.P. Root

I HAVE THE RIGHT...
  Not to justify my existence in this world.
  Not to keep the races separate within me.
  Not to justify my ethnic legitimacy.
  Not to be responsible for people's discomfort with my physical or ethnic ambiguity.

I HAVE THE RIGHT...
  To identify myself differently than strangers expect me to identify.
  To identify myself differently than how my parents identify me.
  To identify myself differently than my brothers and sisters.
  To identify myself differently in different situations.

I HAVE THE RIGHT...
  To create a vocabulary to communicate about being multiracial or multiethnic.
  To change my identity over my lifetime—and more than once.
  To have loyalties and identification with more than one group of people.
  To freely choose whom I befriend and love.

The Painted Victim of a Bleached Society

Jocelyn Loyd

I feel the white snake in my chest
It writhes and coils
Coils and writhes
Tickling my heart with its flickering tongue
Scales like blades rub against my lungs
It tightens its grip whenever I dance
I lose breath when I speak the lingo
And dining on seaweed and rice raises the pressure
I wrap my humid jungle dreams
Placing them into chipped tea cups
Onto a stained cherry wood table
The red, white, and blue blanket
Tangled into my islander hair
I was given mama's wide feet and brown eyes
Now I can walk coast to coast
And see every star fall
Just like a teacher's disappointed smile
When he sees a brown and white stray
Trying to validate her own existence
"I swear I have papa's freckles and light skin"
Yet I'm getting darker each day
Inside and out
You want me to be white
But your precious sun is against you
I am reaching for it everyday
Because that's the biggest star of all
But when I try to climb the palm trees
The snake twists me up a pine
He started off in my chest
But will someday reach my mind
And when that hollow day comes
I'll be the painted victim of a bleached society

Skin

Willa Schneberg

A black woman loans me her skin.
It doesn't fit like a body stocking
or a wetsuit. It becomes mine,
sepia and smooth.

I notice a puncture
on the left side of the torso.
There is blood. My thumb
fits in the slit and finds muscle.

The Band-Aids are the wrong color,
and too small.

I must do something:

unlock her leg irons,
whisk her off the auction block,
shoot the master before he rapes her,
cut down the lynching tree.

Now the woman is in the hallway
wearing her skin. She says,
don't worry, the wound
is always there.

Define Me

Alex Gerald

There's a tree in my yard
An old Dogwood
It's twisted and it's ugly and it's beautiful.
It's actually two trees fused together
But you can only tell when it blooms in the spring
When the flowers choose to start flaunting their pigment
You'll see one half is White and the other half
Is not

See, these days I *hang* my laundry out to dry.
And my house is the perfect distance
From that Dogwood tree
To tie a knot around a sturdy lookin' branch
And unravel a spool of family history across the lawn
To a creaky, leaking gutter
At the base of my roof.
There's a nightgown, an army coat and a Red plaid jacket
On that clothing line
So people can see what I'm made of
Before they try to define me.

Define me.

They used to try to do it to my dad
How Black?
You couldn't be more than half.
Fed up, he used to tell 'em he was Green
Now my father was naive, but I like what he was doin'
Shoulda screamed
I'm not a color, motherfucker!
I'm a human.

Define me.

It's been a steady stream for me since about the sixth grade
No you're not.

Maybe an eighth.
Checking anywhere from one to three boxes
Depending on how the question gets asked
Introductions:
Hey. What's up, man? This is Alex. He's Black.

Define me.

But first let me tell you about my dad's great grandma
Who always used to wear a White nightgown.
I don't know her real name, but they used to call her Othermama.
Othermama smoked till the day she died.
And supposedly
Apparently
She was full-blooded Cherokee
And I saw this old picture of her from back in the day
She was in a rocking chair, rocking 20-inch braids
And she did look pretty damn Cherokee
So I hang her nightgown on that clothing line.

Define me.

Actually...
That reminds me.
Recently
I was digging through a beat up briefcase full of family secrets
And stuck between a couple school pictures and a Polaroid
Was a photograph of my dad's dad.
Grandpa.
We used to call him Pops.
Fought in the Korean War as a young man.
Somewhere along the way he earned a Purple Heart.
And later went on to be an educator.
First Black principal in Oregon, remember?
And this photo

Shows Pops with two little White kids and a little Black kid
And they're all riding hockey sticks like racehorses
And smiling
And laughing
So I laughed, too.
Then I cried
Because I never knew him.
I hang his oversized army coat
On that clothing line.

Define me.

I never got to meet my grandmother, either.
But my dad says she was beautiful and amazing and ahead of her time
The woman had five kids
Two degrees
And a job
Before the clock struck 1969.
And she was African American
And she always used to wear a Red plaid jacket.
It's hanging up with Othermama's nightgown and Pop's coat
On that string
Strung between a gutter and a Dogwood tree
And when my dad met *my* mom
He swears
She was wearing the
Exact
Same
Thing.
Red plaid.
Now this was at Greek Fest.
They were both drunk
So the details are all a little bit iffy
But that's when the background singers started singing

We want the funk
Give up the funk (ow)

And then kids happened.
Catastrophe.

And when I tell people that I'm Black, they
(laughs)
They laugh at me
Like I'm a half-breed, Mulatto, Yellow, high-ass travesty
Like I'm two, fused together
And when I choose to start flaunting my pigment
You'll see one half is White and the other half
Isn't
I'm twisted and I'm ugly and I'm beautiful.

Define me.

The Accidental Racist

Ari Abramovitz

The man stares at me. I'm brown. That's probably the first thing he notices. I'm brown. Looking at the stranger, I see that he's white. "Another one," I chuckle to myself. "They're like rabbits." In Mexico I would be one of the crowd, a drop in a sea of dark skin. Here I stick out like a shark in a swimming pool. And yet I fit in. My clothes are nice, button-up shirts and cardigans; my posture is strong and resolute; my walk is steady and in my hand rests a smartphone. Brown skin with a white boy's clothes. "Goodbye generic white man," I mutter, crossing the street toward the downtown Starbucks. I'm not positive to whom I am speaking.

At Cleveland High School in Southeast Portland—one of the whiter parts of the city—two of my closest friends are also brown. Contrary to popular belief, not all brown is the same. Ponce is Mexican, like myself, while Bauer is Ecuadorian. However, we each have traits that contradict our physical appearance. Ponce was brought up in what he calls a "traditional Mexican household." He is immersed in Latino culture, from the food he eats to the religion his family believes in. On the other hand, Bauer and I are not in touch with that culture. We are what Ponce refers to as "whitewashed." Two Latinos who, rather than observing their own ethnicity, adopt white culture instead. He laughs at us, saying, "You gringos."

Bauer and I have darker skin than Ponce, yet, when it comes down to it, all three of us are in between. Ponce's father is Mexican and his mother is white. Bauer is similar, a white mother and an Ecuadorian father. I am the odd one out in this case as both my parents are Mexican, but I was adopted by a white father. In these ways Bauer and I are more similar through culture and skin tone; Bauer and Ponce are more similar through genetics; Ponce and I are more similar through self-identification; and all three of us belong to the same generic title of Latino. While we may have our differences, we agree that our perceived commonality is comforting.

An accidental racist. The skeleton in my closet. This trait of mine has come from a combination of experiences. The central backbone of it is the constant paradox between Ponce, Bauer, and myself. The ribs are made of the observation of behavior from certain ethnicities and races while the pelvis and legs support the ideas through racist humor. The arms are the ways I reach out to people through my skin color and traits associated with it. The neck turns the head to and fro, taking in some comments about my identification as a Mexican and ignoring others. Finally, the skull is the holder of the brain, eyes, and ears. This is where most thinking and processing happens. The skull stares at my drama teacher as she tells me there is no part for me in Cleveland's production of South Pacific except as one of the Polynesian boys; it listens to my foster brother talk about his loathing of having brown skin, despite him looking white; it thinks about what Ponce means by calling me a white Mexican. This skeleton always raises more questions than it answers. Is this lifestyle habit or choice? Am I a racist for belonging to a white culture but speaking as though I were brought up a Mexican? Can I even call myself a Mexican anymore?

That woman is staring at me. I'm brown. That's probably the first thing she notices about me.

We're all the Same

Cesar Pineda

You profile me as a thug
Small to you as a bug
You profile me as a gangster,
A killer and a no good crook
You arrest me for petty little crimes
And throw me that heavy book
You profile me as a cold-hearted
Crazy type of guy
Abusing your badge's power,
Saying I'm a look-alike, not sly

If you only knew me
I'm just like you, nobody better
Only trying to maintain
I am a hard worker, a mentor, a leader
With a background of heartaches and pain
I'm just trying to let you know we're all the same
So don't call us delinquents or stereotype us
Call us by our names with respect
Like we do, that's all we expect

By Michael Cuauhte'moc Martinez

Just Because

Sean Miles

Just because I'm white
doesn't mean I can't
jump.

Just because I'm white
doesn't mean I'm
racist.

It doesn't mean
I don't have
rhythm

And it doesn't mean I suck at basketball.

I'm not rich
I don't suck at soccer
I'm not scared of black people
And I'm not a redneck.

Just because I'm white doesn't mean
you know
me.

So why do you think you do?

By S. Renee Mitchell

Give Me Some Skin: How I Became White

Patrick McDade

I didn't ask to be born white. It just happened that way. And for the most part of my life, I didn't even know I was white. I knew other people were black, though. And I knew there weren't many black people in my neighborhood. But if you were black, you knew it.

What did I know about myself? I knew I was born in Sacramento, California to an Air Force father and a waitress mother. There was an Air Force base in Tuscan, Arizona, so that's where we lived. By the time I was four my parents were divorced. My mom remarried a carpenter soon after. We were all white, and none of us knew it. Why didn't they tell us?

I knew I was Polish, though. I knew that because it was weird. My mom told me that my family has a partly Polish heritage. I told someone I was Polish, and pretty soon, that's what I was. When you're in school, whatever makes you *weird* is what you *are*. I was a shy, smart boy who liked to hang out with girls, and so I was a little bit proud that I was weird, because I didn't really like the people who weren't. This was in the 70s. If you're reading this and can relate to what I'm saying, you probably agree that not much has changed. But even though I was a weird Polack, who hung around with girls and used big words, I didn't know I was a white Polack.

A white friend asked me once, "How often do you think about your race?"

"Maybe three or four times a week," I told her. I thought I was being honest with myself, admitting that I sometimes think about race, but not enough to be racist. Then she said, "See that black guy over there? How often do you think he thinks about race?"

And then it happened. I turned white.

Actually, that story isn't exactly true. I wish it were. The process of discovering my whiteness, how deep it goes, and how unconscious it is, has been much longer and more meandering. It wasn't my friend who asked me how often I think about race, it was someone else asking someone else, someone white.

This made me realize that everyone's reality is not the same. That it's not a level playing field. That it didn't really change the one who was asked the question. In fact, he went away thinking that black people were *more* racist, because they're just locked into their own way of thinking about themselves as disadvantaged.

Then again, I'm not sure if he went away thinking that. Because I talk about this all the time, I know that white people often say such things about black people. Of course it's not just whites who say that, but people from all backgrounds. And maybe it's even true, in a way. This is a way of blaming people for something that happened to them. Racism today isn't like it used to be. It's not about the active hating, the violence, the lynching, and the slavery. It's about the assumption that white is normal. It's about the deck being stacked.

Something I've learned about my white race is that it's slippery, like all privilege. One way you know you have it is if you don't think you have it. If you don't believe me, try calling everyone by their race--Asian, African American, Mexican, and call white people, "White."

What will happen is that a lot of white people will call you a racist. But the truth is, they want you to protect them from having to think about the fact that they never have to think about their race. That's protecting their privilege—the privilege to walk through life whistling and not having to think about it.

So, I'm trying to stop using the word racism. People get confused about racism. We think that all there is to say is:

"I'm not racist, I think everyone is equal."

Or,

"I'm white, but I never owned any slaves. That black guy hates me because I'm white. That's racist."

Or,

"Why should I say hello to the only black student in my class—if I say hello to her, but I don't say hello to everyone else, isn't that racist because I noticed that she's black?"

The big problem is not the feeling of hatred, which most believe no longer exists in the same way. We forgot to fix the things that make our society treat white as the standard, and everything else as outside it. We have to confront the things that make white skin considered beautiful when black is not. Other stereotypes we have to undo include: That black men are dangerous. White men are just white men, good and bad. Mexicans are hard workers who love God and family. Asians are really smart and quiet. Indians are drunks.

I think white superiority is the new racism. This is *the assumption that being white is normal and everything else is unusual.* It's different than white supremacy, which is an active hatred. In order to not get caught up in the mentality of white superiority, you have to recognize there is an assumption that whiteness is the only norm—and you have to commit to ending it, instead of just pretending it isn't there.

I'm still discovering my whiteness, every single day. Sometimes I hate thinking about race, ethnicity, and skin color. I think about it more than I used to, and I see more of my biases. I'm more aware of biases all around me.

White people need to start seeing other white people. Instead of just seeing who doesn't look like them. As those of us who benefit from being the status quo start to get tired of race, we'll get tired of reminding everyone else of their race as well. Maybe then we can move from "black" and "white" to "black and white."

The Negro Mother

Langston Hughes

Children, I come back today
To tell you a story of the long dark way
That I had to climb, that I had to know
In order that the race might live and grow.
Look at my face—dark as the night—
Yet shining like the sun with love's true light.
I am the dark girl who crossed the red sea
Carrying in my body the seed of the free.
I am the woman who worked in the field
Bringing the cotton and the corn to yield.
I am the one who labored as a slave,
Beaten and mistreated for the work that I gave—
Children sold away from me, I'm husband sold, too.
No safety, no love, no respect was I due.

Three hundred years in the deepest South:
But God put a song and a prayer in my mouth.
God put a dream like steel in my soul.
Now, through my children, I'm reaching the goal.

Now, through my children, young and free,
I realized the blessing deed to me.
I couldn't read then. I couldn't write.
I had nothing, back there in the night.
Sometimes, the valley was filled with tears,
But I kept trudging on through the lonely years.
Sometimes, the road was hot with the sun,
But I had to keep on till my work was done:
I had to keep on! No stopping for me—
I was the seed of the coming Free.
I nourished the dream that nothing could smother
Deep in my breast—the Negro mother.
I had only hope then, but now through you,
Dark ones of today, my dreams must come true:
All you dark children in the world out there,
Remember my sweat, my pain, my despair.

Remember my years, heavy with sorrow—
And make of those years a torch for tomorrow.
Make of my pass a road to the light
Out of the darkness, the ignorance, the night.
Lift high my banner out of the dust.
Stand like free men supporting my trust.
Believe in the right, let none push you back.
Remember the whip and the slaver's track.
Remember how the strong in struggle and strife
Still bar you the way, and deny you life—
But march ever forward, breaking down bars.
Look ever upward at the sun and the stars.
Oh, my dark children, may my dreams and my prayers
Impel you forever up the great stairs—
For I will be with you till no white brother
Dares keep down the children of the Negro Mother.

By Daniel Stauffer

Coffee

Justin McDaniels

Sometimes when I wake up, I enjoy a cup of coffee. Coffee without milk is black and holds a bold flavor, compared to coffee with milk that is brown, strong but soft and creamy. Either way, it's still coffee. The same goes for me, a biracial man with creamy brown skin, given to me by a black father and a white mother. I often find myself in strange predicaments where I am told by friends and peers, "You don't act very black," or "You don't really seem black to me." While I recognize that I have mixed-race parents and don't appear fully *black*, being black is a part of me. It's integral to how I express myself. My physical features have always showcased me as black, and because society categorizes people based on race, I'm rarely considered white.

I never really thought friends telling me I'm *not very black* would be hurtful. Then I recognized what it means. It's like someone telling me that I don't belong, that I'm an alien amongst people I thought I could identify with, when I'm already trying so hard to understand myself. I may not be a straight cup of coffee, but I am proud to have that splash of milk. Being biracial is not bad or strange. I am glad to have these two races make up who I am.

Remembering Race

Cindy Williams Gutiérrez

Race is what runs smoothly in the blood, la sangre—
the stories relayed from generation to generation of la familia.
It manifests not in the color of skin, but in taste—el sabor
de salsa, chocolate, and the tequila, lime, and salt of la fiesta.
I have heard it sleep in the steeple-fingered murmurings of la fe
and then escape again and again on feast days for los Santos.
But who am I to speak of la Raza or pray to merciful saints?
My rubia skin is privileged, my humor sanguine.
What do I need with the bare, stooping shoulders of faith?
The patent sound of Prada heels is all too familiar.
I am not la criada cleaning up the waste of company feasts.
The only race I've run is up the ladder—I savored
the piquant taste of all those falls on my saber.
I was once an expert on that race, trading sanity
for adrenaline—the rush—from hurdling feats.
I swallowed fear like steroids, sweated sang-froid.
No lovers, no children, no filial ties
to monopolize me. I was one of the faithful.
Then one day I forfeited that race. Brazenly unfaithful,
I stepped out on corporate America and tried to save
the lover who was left. I felt no hussy's thrill—
just hunger for the tureens of words I'd gulped down sadly,
and all those old songs I couldn't remember singing.
This was the point of return—when I indulged in a fête
a la Mexicana. I shouted to a grito, *Tell the world I defeated
my enemy.* A victory against blood: my own. On this fateful
day saints welcomed me. Ghosts of old selves sang
as they unloaded memorias at the wharves
of my heart. I tasted the air. It was godly.
I stood rooted in my past. It was earthly.

And now, if I'm lucky, I'll tread lightly on Earth
before she blankets me. I'll look squarely at Death—
look her in the eye—and conjure the Dual God
of my ancestors. More than once I'll trick Fate,
re-enter this race by heeding every cry but those of War.
Then I'll return again and again to the ancient Song.
I'll wear this rosary like a necklace of elders—Santos of my fe.
I may not pray or throw a fiesta, but I'll bite the beads for el sabor—
This salt on my tongue: the taste of familia, blood, la sangre.

Ego Tripping (there may be a reason why)

Nikki Giovanni

I was born in the congo
I walked to the fertile crescent and built
the sphinx
I designed a pyramid so tough that a star
that only glows every one hundred years falls
into the center giving divine perfect light
I am bad
I sat on the throne
drinking nectar with allah
I got hot and sent an ice age to europe
to cool my thirst
My oldest daughter is nefertiti
the tears from my birth pains
created the nile
I am a beautiful woman
I gazed on the forest and burned
out the sahara desert
with a packet of goat's meat
and a change of clothes
I crossed it in two hours
I am a gazelle so swift
so swift you can't catch me
For a birthday present when he was three
I gave my son hannibal an elephant
He gave me rome for mother's day
My strength flows ever on
My son noah built new/ark and
I stood proudly at the helm
as we sailed on a soft summer day
I turned myself into myself and was
jesus
men intone my loving name
All praises All praises
I am the one who would save
I sowed diamonds in my back yard
My bowels deliver uranium

the filings from my fingernails are
semi-precious jewels
On a trip north
I caught a cold and blew
My nose giving oil to the arab world
I am so hip even my errors are correct
I sailed west to reach east and had to round off
the earth as I went
The hair from my head thinned and gold was laid
across three continents
I am so perfect so divine so ethereal so surreal
I cannot be comprehended except by my permission
I mean...I...can fly
like a bird in the sky...

©1968 Nikki Giovanni

Melva Perez with her favorite poet, Nikki Giovanni
By Kate McPherson

Lost

Miranda Mendoza

A child
Born of three worlds.
From the mixture of the EnGer Jew (English, German, Jewish)
And the beauty of the Flor de Mega
To the Pearl of the Orient.

She is small
But a formidable foe
Like an angry cobra
Ready to strike at any intruders.

"The daughter of Aphrodite,"
Said her mother over and over
"Girls wish they had your beauty..."

Lips blood-red
Brown eyes dark and vivacious
Hair so wavy and so thick it is
The envy of the oceans.

Light as her mother
But her father denied her
The love she deserved and desperately wanted.
Because of her skin
He believed that the child was not his
So he never smiled.

A child
Who never understood her background
Is in a world where people
Want to know.

They want to know
About her culture.
They want to know
About her history.
They want to know about her heritage.

All she can say
Is that she is a person
She is she
And that is all that matters.

"Being Brown" by Jen Wick, courtesy of Oregon Humanities.

White Guilt

S. Renee Mitchell

if yre waiting on reparations
u better go on and let that rest
u can't depend on the white man's conscience
to raise up black consciousness
everything I got I earned
everything I want to know I learn
my success is up to me
I think independently
'cause white guilt
don't sign my paycheck

I've heard it said
that to keep blacks ignorant
all yve got to do is write it down in a book
well u can call me an intellectual pirate
for all the knowledge that I took
I'm spinning truth into rhymes
griot of hope in a troubled time
asking young minds
    what's the name of the last book u read
'cause no one can steal what's in yr head
& it's not what they call u but what u answer to
& learning's not over until yr life is through
now I'm not trying to tell u what to do
but I am trying to break it down for u
& remind u what Martin Luther King Jr. meant
when he said
    Nobody can ride u my brothers & sisters
    unless yr back is bent

how can we be satisfied
when equal rights are still a mystery
black children don't know their history
society is window dressing misery
putting justice for the colored on a 50-percent-off sale
yet u think oppression is over
cause a black man is in the white house
while rolling on dubs in your SUVs
please!
we may look like rich dark chocolate
but our history still tastes bittersweet
& though those slave chains are broken
we are still intrinsically linked

can u hear our ancestors moaning
all proud regal & fine
they all may have gone home
but they left crumbs behind
so we cannot lose our way
to that great promised land
but we are not there yet
now do u understand
what I am trying to say
souls without footsteps need u
to step up & march on
the rest of the way
so step up
my brothers & sisters
stand up
speak up

so the next time yre wondering
about that thought u just had
it was a whisper from Martin saying
My dreams are not dead

that space between anger
& u lifting yr fist
is Malcolm's spirit reminding u
Brother, I didn't die for this

that painful wince u got watching
music videos promoting hip-hop
that have naked black behinds
shaking non-stop
was Sojourner Truth telling u to get up
& turn that mess off

entertainment has its place
& we all like it so much
rappers, singers & dancers
make us feel like we've been touched
but what have u done
to live yr life out loud
what have u done
to make yr great grandchildren proud

so when u get through
dancing and prancing from the latest tunes
when u've grown tired
of groaning, moaning
singing the blues
what kind of a legacy will u leave behind u
we cannot wait for white guilt
to deliver us affirmative action
hand out reparations, satisfaction
appease us with don imus
or trent lott-styled retractions
we need passion
& not just the kind
that makes us more babies
we need to birth a revolution
we need to save we

I stand up straight
I decide my fate
I speak up against hate
ain't afraid to set u straight
cause white guilt
don't sign my paycheck

Religion

This is my simple religion. There is no need for temples; no need for complicated philosophy. Our own brain, our own heart is our temple; the philosophy is kindness.

Dalai Lama

Just as a candle cannot burn without fire, men cannot live without a spiritual life.

Buddha

The Red Road to Home

Brenda Reyes

I remember the day my life changed. November 2011–I was invited for a Day of the Dead celebration in the St. John's neighborhood. I went with my family without knowing what to expect. When I first heard the drum I couldn't resist moving my feet. That's when I fell in love with percussion, the music we all learn in the womb of our mothers. The drum represents the heart of the mother.

Before things improved, I was drowning in my own pain. I didn't know what it meant to be loved, to pray, to receive the good of life. I think this is because from a young age I was vulnerable to the forces around me. One of them was alcohol, which I did not consume voluntarily. It followed me as a disgusting habit. I never had much of a childhood. I was deeply hurt by a person I trusted, someone I considered family. I was angry and lost. By the end of eighth grade, I decided I was going to give up on school, and on life, completely.

The expression, "education is the key to success," woke me from the dark sleep that was my life. I found it inside a fortune cookie. In April of 2012, I took my first step onto the Red Road to the Native American Church. I became one of the proud women in the circle of La Danza Azteca, Xochipilli. After three months of Danza, I was in a sacred place. My body became my temple, and I no longer had any desire for alcohol. I've worked and dedicated my time and life to these precious ways, and shown respect to everyone and everything, just like my father taught me. This has earned me the respect of my community. And of myself.

The following year, my sister Sophia was born five weeks premature. She was barely able to breathe on her own. We couldn't even take her home from the hospital, and didn't know what would happen. It seemed like she was dying, little by little. I was also struggling. How could I balance summer school, this new tragedy, and being a mother to my siblings as well as my own mother? I took all the pain in my heart and went to Danza. I wanted to be another dead leaf blowing in the wind. That night my native sister, Desiree, saw the pain in me. She prayed over the water for Sophia.

My entire Lakota family had also prayed for my sister and, on the third day of their prayers, my sister was able to breathe on her own and come home! I will never forget that day–the prayers that changed my faith. It changed the people I see as family, who cared enough to keep me standing on my own feet. The prayer showed me that water is life, as it brought my sister back to life. Now I have the ability, the gift to connect with my people. I'm learning the ways of my ancestors and a healthy new way to live with love and hope.

I could say hundreds of beautiful things of my journey on the Red Road, but you have to experience it to understand. It has humbled me. I have a new family to replace my past, broken family. I would not have been able to face those troubles alone, and I am no longer alone. My new family is teaching the right words; I make them actions; they change my life.

My name is Brenda Reyes-Nunez and I came into this world sixteen years ago. I am a part of La Danza Azteca, Xochipilli, and the Native American Church. I have been sober since October 2012 and will continue to be. I formally brought M.E.Ch.A back to Roosevelt High School to increase Latino involvement in my community. I am not a victim of my past because I refuse to label myself that way. As hard as my journey was, and will be, it will keep teaching me how to better myself.

I Didn't Ask for This.

Brooke Perry

Half of my childhood was lived as a pastor's kid, while the other half consisted of a distance, both physical and spiritual, thick with doubt about the church and the God we worshipped. My dad passed away, and my family's faith went with him.

Since my childhood called it quits, I have been doing everything in my power to be good enough for God. I have consistently fallen deeper in love with Him over the past twelve years, and parallel with that, have had a consistent disdain for that love.

I have said, more often than I care to admit, "I didn't ask for this." I've had this odd resentment of being raised to know such deep truth and love that I will never be able to escape it. I never wanted to be the weird girl who felt convicted about messing around with boys, drinking or smoking. I hated that Jesus never left my heart. I hated that I had to feel guilty for things that others merely glanced at as they ran headfirst into deeper "sins" than I was committing.

I never asked to love Jesus, and I had a consistent battle going on in my heart between being incredibly overwhelmed by the love I felt from Him (and feeling completely insane about that overwhelming feeling), and hating that I couldn't get away from this love.

The worst part is, I love Him back! I can't help it! It's a deeper love than I have ever known in my entire life, and try as I did, and I *did and do*, I couldn't deny that my heart, inevitably, was His.

And yet He didn't force it from me.

I can *want* Him to have my heart with the very depths of my soul, and yet, He doesn't pry it from my hands, He waits for me to freely give it to Him.

...and then *lets me take it back*

...and then waits patiently as I crawl back to Him and surrender it once again.

I started going back to church when I was in junior high. Where the urging came from I'm still not sure, but the part of me that still believes in a sovereign God believes it was Him. I could have just heard about a cute boy attending though. I honestly don't remember.

What I do remember is the immediate desire I had to return. Throughout junior high I attended this youth group and got incredibly involved, and fell in love with Jesus all over again.

We all long for meaning, purpose and influence. Hell, most of us would probably just settle with *someone* having *something* nice to say about us at our funeral someday.

At least that's how I feel most of my days.

And right behind those desires in my heart, the voices in my head are on repeat until all I can hear sometimes is:

Is God happy with me? What do I need to ask for forgiveness for? Do those people think I'm good enough to serve Jesus? Do those people know how incapable I am of serving Jesus? Do I look fat in this shirt? Am I worth her love? Am I trying too hard? Am I not trying hard enough? Am I lazy?

Do I matter?

    Do I care if I matter?

        Will my heart ever come through?

        Is my heart good?

            Are my intentions bad?

                How will I ever be good enough?

And then that defiance comes back, I *didn't ask for this.*

And I start to resent Jesus once again. I start to long for naiveté, for a shallow life. For one that doesn't ask all of these questions. For one that doesn't mean this much. Then there would be a lot less pressure, right?

Most of my life that I can remember I have served God. I have served the church, His Church. And this is truly one of the deepest passions of my soul (whether I wanted it to be or not). I have served the needy, the poor, the underprivileged. I find true joy out of leading others into serving. I find true calling and purpose in being a part of a team who serves Jesus together and tries to give others the identity that Christ has called them into, which is supposed to be an identity of *freedom and feeling loved.*

And then I realized I felt anything but free or loved.

And then everything came crashing down.

And to my genuine surprise, as humbling as that is to admit, Jesus was the only strong, tall, sturdy pillar standing amongst the rubble of my life.

In the pursuit of identity and purpose *in Christ* I had placed people, service, relationships and His own church in front of the very God that I "represented" in all of these areas of my life.

By doing that I had completely lost who I was in doing things for Him or for my "religion." And as each one of these things came to a crashing halt and I was stripped of everything and everyone that I have ever really truly deeply loved, I felt exposed, vulnerable and weak. I had no idea where to turn, what to do, or how I was going to ever be able to look at myself in the mirror again.

I had nothing that I had ever defined myself by. I had nothing in which I had found worth or purpose anymore.

And yet I was still breathing. Granted, most of those breaths were grasped between gut-wrenching sobs, but the breathing remained: inconsistent, shallow at times, but life-sustaining.

My lungs stretched out and contracted back, providing air that sustained my life. And in the same way, the Holy Spirit was stretching and contracting back in my very soul to provide some of the deepest and most real breaths into my heart and into my faith that I had ever taken.

In a moment where I literally felt I was losing everything, I realized Jesus was the only place I could ever find my true identity, and therefore my true purpose. That it was by everything *about Him* falling away that I finally saw the most real glimpse *of Him* that I have ever seen.

See, my faith doesn't just shape who I am, *it is the very essence of my existence.* Even things *about* my faith poison the true meaning of how my faith in itself is my very identity.

I identify with Jesus. The further away He is and the more that is in between Him and me means that there is just as much in between my identity and my self.

The longing in my soul to please Him was the very barrier that kept me from realizing that all He wants in order to be happy with me is, well, just *me*.

So I guess instead of being able to answer how my faith shapes my sense of identity, I think the truer question for me is: How is there any clarification of identity without my faith? There is no line there to me. They are one in the same. Everything else is just an act to try and place an identity on myself that looks "right." One that fits in with…something, anything.

Instead, I strive now to drop the act, and to let Him place *His* identity into the core of my soul so that even when everything about me is wrong, people will see the only right thing about me, which is Jesus Christ Himself dwelling inside of my heart.

By Christe Jackson

Third Chance

Jake Peru-Bass

I am from Top Ramen
From plastic chairs
But endless toys
I am from the duplex
With the small shed and driveway
It sounded loud
The banging on the door
The cop that says, "Open the fucking door!"
I am from fear
Fear of losing my father
Fear of the authorities
Not even seven years old

Thirteen with no dreams
I am from fear of being taken
From the ones I learned to hate
I am from street fights
From guns blasting
And the knife that struck my back
I am from, "So what?"
And, "You aren't shit!"
I am from hopelessness
From broken promises
From messed up relationships
From my mother and my father
I am from missed opportunities
To teach my sister the right thing to do

Fifteen now
A regained path
And a new light
I can say I came from the bottom
I came from probable death
And wrongdoings
To finding God
A god that is giving me a third chance
My third chance of life
A chance I will use
To make it up to my parents
And to teach my sister the right thing to do

The Hijab

Qanani Kalil

I have been wearing the hijab since I was in the fifth grade. Every morning, I would place a thin, colorful silk scarf over my coarse hair, and attempt to wrap it perfectly around my head. It would take me ages to fit it right. The knots would come undone, the folds would unfold and wisps of hair would secretly escape. I used to watch my mother in awe, as; with a flick of her hand she could wrap a scarf around her head, flawlessly.

Although the hijab is obligatory in my religion, that is not the only reason why I began wearing it. In fact, no one told me that it was mandatory. Many women wore it, including my friends and family from my homeland, Ethiopia. I was elated to be one of them, and experience it for the first time. I felt more confident and mature, and as happy as a songbird singing at the rising of the sun. To this day each time I walk out of the house in my hijab, I feel like angels are smiling down upon me, a sure sign that God is happy. I thought of the hijab as the most beautiful accessory I owned, more beautiful than my necklaces, earrings and wooden hair clips. But it is more than a color, shape, or material.

As I grew older, I came to realize that the hijab was not merely an accessory, but a meaningful symbol with an important message. The hijab is a symbol of respect, confidence, beauty, and a Muslim woman's willingness to dutifully follow her religion. I believe it is what makes me who I am. It helps to shape, mold, and construct me into a unique human being.

I view the hijab as a symbol of my freedom. One might think the opposite, that the hijab is oppressive, and Muslim women must cover their hair because they are not liberated. I wear the hijab trusting that people will not judge me by my physical appearance, like whether or not I have a good hair day. I hope they will be judging me in the words of Martin Luther King Jr. "...by the content of their (my) character." People accept and appreciate me for who I am, hijab and all. Hence, wearing the hijab has made me free.

I moved to the United States in 2006, and was surprised and a bit terrified to see few people wearing the hijab. Because of this, I used to have difficulty wearing mine in public. Regardless of my love and respect for the hijab, one cannot deny that it differentiates a female from others in society. Sometimes I feel very self-conscious. I am among the only Muslims at my high school, and I'm the only one who wears the hijab, which makes me feel out of place in the student population. Sometimes I even get degrading looks. However, I am determined to be as brave as a warrior and not give up on the hijab, as some other Muslimahs have. Rather than giving up, I am further motivated to continue following the traditions of my religion.

To others, the hijab is a mere scarf wrapped around one's head. For me, it is a representation of freedom and religious beliefs. The colors are like my emotions: black for a somber mood and yellow for a joyous one. The materials reflect the temperature of my body: wool for a colder day, and silk for a warmer one. These are a few, among many other reasons, as to why I love the hijab. I will not be hurt by what ignorant people say about my decision to wear it. Forever proud to be a hijab-wearing Muslimah, I will continue to wear it and never wish to stop.

Identify Our Oneness

Arun Toke

"Who are you?" people often ask me.

"I am Arun, born and raised in India. I am an Indian American, an Asian American citizen. I speak Marathi, a language from western India," I say with an accent.

I might add further, "I am a born-again, Unitarian Universalist Hindu, a student of life. I am a vegetarian, a non-smoker, a 'teetotaler,' a health-nut, a nature-lover, and an activist."

When they ask for more I say, "I'm an ex-engineer, and an editor of Skipping Stones, an international, nonprofit, multicultural magazine based in Eugene, Oregon. I started it some 25 years ago to promote cultural and linguistic diversity, international understanding and nature awareness. We publish student writing, art and photos from all over the world."

Depending on my mood, I might ramble on, "I am a world-traveler, a global citizen. I'm on a lifelong journey."

I want people to like me, and so I tell things about me that they might like. If they belong to a Spanish-speaking culture, I try to stretch what little skills I have in Spanish. I might talk about my 3,000 km bicycle trip in Northern Europe, or a marathon that I ran many years ago. I try to show that we have many things in common.

Deep down, I want everyone to maintain their cultural, ethnic identities and religious traditions, and at the same time, embrace the diversity of our global family. While treasuring our own heritage, language, culture, religion, family, and experiences, we can still venture out of our cultural, national or religious cocoons.

I am not just a Hindu, Indian, or a father. I am not my pride or ego. I am none of these worldly labels and identities. I am a human being, or should I say, a living being. I want to respect all living things in the world... not just human beings. Even ants, flies, and spiders deserve our respect. We are all interconnected. In fact, we are so interconnected that Amma, my spiritual teacher, says, "Children, you cannot harm anyone without injuring yourself, nor can you help anyone without benefiting yourself."

Let us realize the Oneness of all living beings now. Let's begin by developing the awareness of our unity *now*. Let's walk in each other's shoes, feel their pains and joys, points of views, and let's treat others as we wish them to treat us.

Spark

From a little spark may burst a flame.

Dante Alighieri

The spark divine dwells in thee: let it grow.

Ella Wheeler Wilcox

O Identity, What Art Thou?

Doc Macomber

O identity, identity wherefore art thou identity?

A mere measure of man, woman, child, or beast?

How so we, O identity, want to prove self, define self, understand self, yet the probing be done so by others.

O identity do I mold, strive, bend to societal winds in vain—O identity, these wicked ways in which we seek to discover, to unbind trueness in time of turmoil.

O identity, do I become a brave soldier, a professional athlete, a nurse, a doctor, a gambler, a saint, a pest terminator…why so strive we, O identity? Is planning by God this? Or something impregnated from conception—a whimsical notion from mountaintops of time beginning or unearthed crustaceans from the seven seas? O God what is thine identity?

Wherefore then when time descend that seek we fame, fortune, happiness—does this, the desire, become our tombstone on which we carve identity?

Great men and women, past or present, O identity, what is that which sets apart thee from the rest? Is it identity, O identity? Or fervent labor or passion gone wild that blazes in soul? That think they, in the wee hours of waylay, something personal as O identity? Do really they the time to ponder then, O identity?

These great honorable people do they, O identity, upon wake, cradle coffee in hand, say, *Today, I'm a brilliant scientist, a renowned poet, a feared politician, a warrior. That this, I am for all eternity. And for all to know of me.*

Never change, will I, O identity. Wherefore I sway never under moments of doubt. Wherefore I admit never visions, which do not match reality.

O identity, do I walk upon bathroom mirror seeking reflection of parent, or both, or parents of, or parents past, only then to find, but intangible faces of action heroes?

O identity, identity where art thou?

O what art thou?

The Pen is as Mighty as the Paintbrush

Abby Pasion

Writing has played an essential role in my life. It's a way for me to express the thoughts or dreams or desires of mine that I cannot with pastels, music or everyday speech. With writing, I take my time to think about the words I'm about to craft. And when I'm done—whether it's a speech, a story, a script, an essay, a poem—I feel I've created something distinct, something elegant, in its eloquence. Writing is what makes me feel the most comfortable; being surrounded by literature (both modern and classic) is like forming new friendships or relationships with the characters you meet. (And the ones you create). To me, it's one of the most beautiful mediums of art in the world.

Football Life

Mendel Miller

My name is Mendel Miller, a lineman for the Roosevelt Roughriders. Football is my home, my everything. I love everything about the sport—the physical contact, the sweat, loud noises.

Playing football releases all my inner demons. I've now realized that I need football like a baby needs a blankie.

My love for football is like a human's love for water... "Looks like a football life for me."

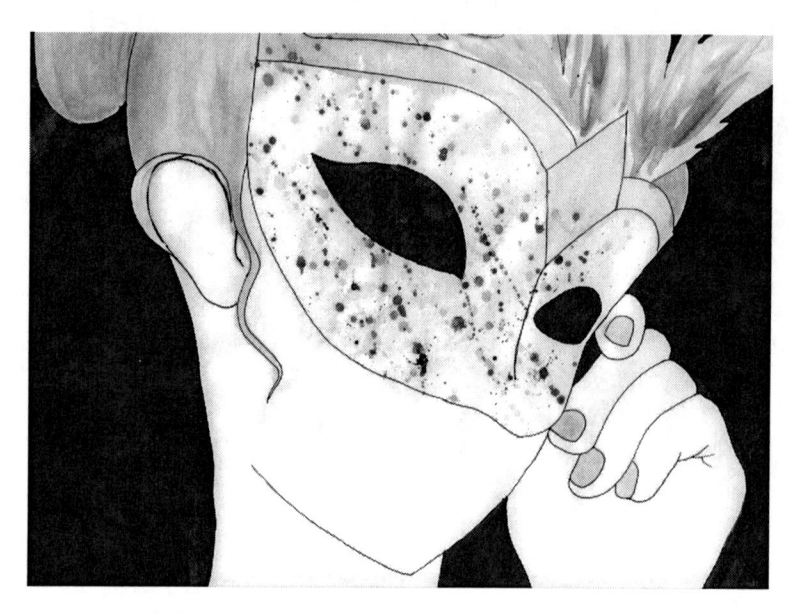

By Anonymous

The Curtain

Devin St. John

The curtain, the only thing that separates the real world from the painted world. I stand behind it, taking in deep breaths as I prepare myself for the performance I am about to give. The parting of the curtain is my signal; I walk out on stage, not as who I was born, but as someone else. A mask covers my body, making me appear as a lone village peasant selling goods from my farm, and until the lead approaches me, I am not at all important to the play.

As the curtain closes and the stage is being set for the next scene, I prepare myself with another mask, this time as an old woman. I am the lead's grandmother as I hobble out onto the stage. The audience may have seen me as a village peasant in the previous scene, but I am always the grandmother and I am always the peasant. At that very moment I lead two lives, wear two masks; I am two people yet one at the same time. As an actor, I am required to switch masks at any moment.

As the final scene begins, I put on one last mask. This time, I am one of the nobles in a royal gathering. My characters' purpose is different than the others for there is something I am trying to hide from the lead. Only a few people know what I am hiding and I prefer to keep it that way. When I am discovered, my mask twists into the shape of a vile and cruel noble who wants nothing but people to respect him.

As the play ends, I put away my masks and go out on stage for that final bow where I then show everyone who I really am. There is no more need for masks anymore, we are now who we were born as. I walk backstage and change back into my normal, everyday clothes. I look back and once again see that thin veil that separates the real world from the painted world, known simply as the curtain.

By Blake Stellye

My Basketball Life

DaLony Armstrong

It was the third overtime; there were twenty seconds left on the clock. Our team was losing 66-61 and we needed to steal the ball. I stole the ball and threw it like a baseball to my teammate Adam to make the lay-up. The score was now 66-63 and we were down three points. My teammate Jacob made a three-pointer and he got fouled. The game was tied 66-66; Jacob made his free throws to win the game 67-66!

Basketball is my favorite hobby. I live across the street from my middle school's basketball courts where we play full-court five on five or one on one whenever we want.

Playing on varsity made me feel like Michael Jordan winning a championship.

Passion for the Action

Melissa Vang

I could feel my heart race like someone running nonstop to a marathon. I inhale deeply then exhale out, ready and focused. As I serve the ball up high, I pull back my right arm, spreading my fingers out wide to tighten my palms. I take a step back, using all my mighty strength. As the ball is in the air twirling like a ballerina in her tutu, I freely swing my arm and smack the ball toward the net. It makes it over. I feel the relief that was inside of me as if I just came out of the shower refreshed. Now the game has really begun.

The Choir

Vikram Srinivasan

I grew up in southern India's bustling city of Chennai. In 2002, I headed to the USA to attend graduate school. A few years later, I moved to Portland for my first job. Not having a clue about this "white" city—its bohemian culture and quirky identity—made the transition an intimidating experience. Especially as an immigrant, a person of color and a gay man.

That was only in the beginning. Almost immediately after I moved, I joined the Portland Gay Men's Chorus (PGMC)—one of the best decisions of my life. For a choir that was predominantly white men (and some women) from all walks of life, its members were so warm and welcoming that I felt they'd been expecting me the whole time.

Very soon, I made several new friends who have since become an integral part of my life. They carried me on their shoulders when life was unkind, they rushed to my side at a moment's notice; they even helped me move. From them, I learned what acceptance and unconditional support truly means. With them, I saw myself paying their kindness forward when I welcomed new members.

Through music, we became a powerful voice in the community, fighting discrimination and affirming the worth of all. When I notice gay youth coming out to their families at our concerts, it humbles me that I can help others in need while I continue to take those steps for myself.

If an immigrant like me can call Portland home, it is thanks to groups like the PGMC, which prove that you *can* choose family and find a home away from home in a city that keeps community close to its heart.

By Alex Alvarez

A Thousand Words

Julio Lopez

Being a photographer is my passion. I like to capture beautiful moments in pictures so they can last forever. I love nature each time I see a wonderful sighting. I like to share this world's beauty with everyone. Sunrises signify that it's another wonderful day... Being a photographer lets you express yourself in your own ways, sharing what you love with other people.

On Stage

Allissa Purkapile

I love music. I love playing it. I love listening to it. Music runs through my body like my blood runs through my veins. Without music, my life would be off balance because music changes my mood and keeps me calm, even on my craziest days.

    I can play almost any drum. My heart beats as fast as I play my drums. My drumming is intense and I have proven that I am more than what people think. They thought that just because I was a girl, that I could not play as well as a boy could. But I proved them wrong. Me and my music—we are one and the same. We both refuse to stay quiet. We both want to get a message out. We are just heard in a different way.

The Trinity Seesaw

C.J. Rue

Club-footed I am a Cubist.
Bold boxes and squares
show light in a particular way.
Stomach numb
and heavy with satire
I am Picasso.

Smooth like sand to glass
you round the corner
to show us the light.
Soft and harsh pulls our heart
into the submission of beauty.
You are Monet.

Warmth exudes like morning,
waking me up
when I need to.
Push and pull wraps around my soul
to form meaning.
She is art.

By Alissa Ouansisouk

My First Love

Alissa Ouanesisouk

Bright light blinding my eyes. A dark crowd—and the audience's eyeballs staring at me. Voices roared through me.

It was the SUN School showcase at James John Elementary School and I, Alissa Ouanesisouk, was in the break dancing class. It was everyone's first performance and we all had to perform.

As the curtains opened the audience cheered for us. I felt their voices go through my eardrums and it went into my heart. My fingers were trembling like chandeliers in an earthquake and sweat started to flow through my hands.

Then the crowd started to get quiet and was ready to watch us. Once the music started playing my heart dropped, it was time for me to start. As nervous as I was I knew this was a safe place and I could dance no matter what, I had to believe in myself.

Once it was my turn to dance I moved with all my energy. Pushing every step to the furthest and breaking every single sweat possible. With every single movement I had the crowd rooting for me. I realized that as I was dancing I forgot all about the audience and nothing really mattered to me.

My heart punched in my chest and music flowed into my soul pushing every movement out.

After the performance people cheered for us. We all bowed and left the stage. The feeling of relief that it was finally over overtook me.

From that day on I knew dancing was right for me. The beat, the melody, the support from the audience and the movements, that's what I fell in love with. The way I can express my feelings through dance makes dancing my true passion. For my future, I seek more dancing, more practicing, and more motivation in life. I know I can do better.

The summer interns.
By Jeri Lee and Megan Lorenz

Thoughts and Reflections

The Summer Interns

As we reviewed our submissions we had an opportunity to step back to explore what was really valuable about this collection of work. We realized the most of these works are strong and lonely calls for being genuinely known. This urgent need to be heard is shared by all of us —regardless of race, ethnicity, age and gender.

This often feels most urgent for us as teens because we are required to navigate the conflicting expectations of our peers, schools, cultural and spiritual communities, families and our selves. Trying to understand and please all these varied expectations is very confusing and to find one's personal voice can be challenging. It is oddly comforting to know that this sense of conflict is experienced by everyone. We hope these readings and art will enable you, our readers, to embrace this space of conflict so we and the adults in our lives can relax more, feel more at home with this process, and replace tension and urgency with greater harmony.

We formulated a few thoughts and suggestion we think will help youth, parents, and teachers become stronger allies in this journey. We hope the reader will have conversations with others about these ideas and begin to formulate their own recommendations.

What Our Peers Need to Know

- Developing your identity is a process filled with struggle, frustration and drama. It is not a bad thing to be lost or hurt. It is part of the process. Accept it. No pain, no gain.
- Find positive role models whom you can look to for guidance.
- Seek friends who have your back.
- Seek organizations that can nurture you spiritually, morally, and culturally.
- Just because you are biracial does not mean you have to choose between your two cultures.
- Being different is a gift, not a curse.
- Watch what you say.
- Break the cycle and be careful not to spread negative stereotypes.

What Our Parents Need to Know

- Disagreeing does not mean disrespect.
    - Contemporary U.S. culture encourages authentic questioning/youth voice.
    - Youth need to share "respectfully."/Parents need to "hear" their children.
- As teens, we need to "push back" to define and own our personal identity in order to become independent.
- We need time to process—instead of "text me now" say "text me when you get a chance."
- We need to know that we are loved and valued during the development process. This can be shown by:
    - Cooking our favorite food
    - Giving us words of encouragement and love
    - Creating a safe place to voice our feelings
    - Support when we need it, and leaving us alone when we don't
    - Respecting our privacy
- We can feel awkward/even devalued at times. Be aware of that.
- It is often hard for us to see acts of parenting as love.
- If your child is biracial, show them the best of both worlds. Don't make them feel like they have to choose.
- Find adults to mentor and support us. You can't do it alone. Find someone who has similar interests as us and whose personality is more aligned with ours.
- Try to include us in decisions that directly affect us.
- Youth want to embrace both cultures of their families. We want to become part of the contemporary culture of city and school at the same time.

What Our Teachers Need to Know

- Students experience the pressure of multiple expectations:
    - Family roles and expectations
    - Academics
    - Social issues
- You need to encourage students but not overwhelm them.
- Students want to embrace being part of the community's culture as well as part of their own cultures and ethnicities.
- Examples of successful people need to include people with disabilities, or who are adopted, multiracial, LGBT, etc.
- Don't focus on just one student.
- Don't assume students know "their" history.
- Be sensitive towards all cultural/ethnic groups.
- Respect individuality—don't stereotype.
- Talk about culture.
    - Ask about activities/experiences.
    - Ask about family events and traditions.
- Cultural roots—second and third generations are not as versed in cultural history.
    - Don't assume that students know some things and don't know other things.
- Use texting and email.
- Enunciate names.
- Form relationships with your students by:
    - Conversations
    - Saying hello in the hallways
    - Checking emails and texts

Acknowledgements

Thanks to our Supporters and Advisors

The student leaders of Roosevelt's Unique Ink would like to thank all the students and community members who have made this book possible. More than fifty authors as well as professional and student photographers and artists contributed their work.

Portland State University's Ooligan Press serves as our core partner, providing a summer internship and college mentors for our students.

Special thanks to Dennis Stovall, who devoted his summer to guiding our young interns through the complex beginning stages of publishing. Not only did he share his time, he shared a wealth of knowledge which we feel honored and privileged to have learned. His experience in the publishing world helped us to gain a clear sense of what message we wanted to send with this publication. Also, thanks to Per Henningsgaard, who has continually helped us through all phases of our project, even extending into the school year. We are grateful for his willingness to be a part of this project, which wouldn't be possible without his participation.

Provided funding support for the printing of our book:

State Farm

Tim & Mary Boyle

Neighborhood House has provided transportation for our interns and students.

In addition, many community members have also stepped forward to help us develop distribution partnerships and innovative ways to market and sell the book.

Thank you!

An Open Invitation to Community Writers and Artists

We extend an invitation to our readers to submit to our future projects. You can learn about them and find our guidelines at our website: www.rooseveltroughwriters.org.

Please send your questions and feedback to: rhswritingcenter@gmail.com.

Become a Community Ally

This venture will thrive only with the support of community allies to help us with book distribution and marketing, graphic design, social marketing and program financial development. We invite community members, college students, and retirees to step forward to share their skills and time. We guarantee your time will be well spent.

In addition, you can support the Writing and Publishing Center by making a donation, becoming a distribution partner, or serving on one of our project teams.

For more information on these opportunities, visit our website: www.rooseveltroughwriters.org/donate/

or email us at: rhswritingcenter@gmail.com

All proceeds from the sale of this book support Roosevelt's Writing and Publishing Center

Summer Interns

Roosevelt High School

Nathan Buckland
Elizabeth Elia
Jeremy Hogeweide
Matthew Hughes
Miranda Mendoza
Melva Perez
Bovianna Somsanouk
Anthony Sylvester
Brenda Tirado
Doua Vang

Ooligan Press

Sarah Currin
Melissa Gifford
Rebekah Hunt
Margaret Schimming

Summer Internship Advisors

Dennis Stovall
Per Henningsgaard

Publishing Center Coordinator

Kate McPherson

CPSIA information can be obtained
at www.ICGtesting.com
Printed in the USA
FFOW04n0144241217
44167885-43553FF